Becoming a Great School

Praise for *Becoming a Great School*:

"All I can say is WOW. . . . This book includes proven strategies to assist educational leaders to move their schools to the highest levels of excellence. Administrators and faculty in colleges and universities with educational leadership and certification programs should read and then share this book with students in those programs."
—Dr. Bill Osborne, Professor and Dean of Education Emeritus, East Central University, Ada, OK

"A MUST READ for insight into a powerful, proven, successful blueprint to: empower and challenge faculty; enrich school culture and curriculum; and improve test scores with no significant impact on budgets. Pick up the gauntlet and embark on an exciting win-win journey that will benefit America's greatest resource, our children!"
—Donna Dilts, teacher (for 37 years), Doyon School, Ipswich, MA

"Being part of the Doyon School Community under the leadership of Dr. Kenneth Cooper was a personal and professional honor. The inclusive empowerment that he genuinely cultivated gave us all the opportunity to successfully collaborate, lead and grow as life-long learners. Our fourteen school working values fostered such a rewarding, respectful workplace and promoted learning excellence for our students, staff and community members."
—Judith A. Ferrara, Doyon School Teacher & Ipswich Educators Association Building Representative

"*Becoming a Great School* provides a unifying vision for harnessing human potential and creating a caring culture which leads to good choices. I found the book to be organized in a very accessible and useful format that can not only be read in sequence but which one could refer back to as specific sections are relevant. It offers practical advice grounded in research and experience and could be used by both leaders and team members in and out of school settings."
—Dr. Meryl Goldman, adjunct professor St. John's River State College (retired), past president St. John's County Education Foundation

"*Becoming a Great School* is a compelling and insightful book; it demonstrates how school administrators can evolve into leaders who are successful agents of change, creating systemic improvements in their schools. The reader is guided through strategic elements of collaboration, motivation, innovation, and transformation that ultimately benefit the students, enabling them to be well-prepared 21st century learners. This book is essential reading for school leaders who want to revitalize their schools, cultivating a culture of excellence through a collaborative leadership approach."
—Cynthia M. Manning, Principal, Learning Prep High School, West Newton, MA

"As the new Superintendent of the Ipswich Public Schools, the first thing I did was to speak with about 175 persons in the District about the schools. The remarkable culture of the schools came shining through those conversations. It is the kind of professional, enthusiastic, collaborative, 'can do' culture that is often written about in education reform literature but rarely found in operation in a school district."
—Dr. William Hart, Superintendent of the Ipswich Public Schools

May 2014

To Julia

*With gratitude for your
Many years of wonderful guidance
& support of the Cooper clan.*

All the best —

Ken

Becoming a Great School

*Harnessing the Powers of Quality
Management and Collaborative
Leadership*

Kenneth B. Cooper,
Nels Gustafson,
and Joseph G. Salah

ROWMAN & LITTLEFIELD EDUCATION
A division of
ROWMAN & LITTLEFIELD
Lanham • Boulder • New York • Toronto • Plymouth, UK

Published by Rowman & Littlefield Education
A division of Rowman & Littlefield
4501 Forbes Boulevard, Suite 200, Lanham, Maryland 20706
www.rowman.com

10 Thornbury Road, Plymouth PL6 7PP, United Kingdom

British Library Cataloguing in Publication Information Available

Library of Congress Cataloging-in-Publication Data

Cooper, Kenneth B., 1946–
Becoming a great school : harnessing the powers of quality management and collaborative leadership / Dr. Kenneth B. Cooper, Nels Gustafson, and Joseph G. Salah.
pages cm.
Includes bibliographical references and index.
ISBN 978-1-4758-0694-6 (cloth : alk. paper) — ISBN 978-1-4758-0695-3 (pbk. : alk. paper) — ISBN 978-1-4758-0696-0 (electronic) 1. School improvement programs. 2. Total quality management. I. Gustafson, Nels, 1943– II. Salah, Joseph G., 1941– III. Title.
LB2822.8.C68 2013
371.2'07—dc23
2013036591

♾™ The paper used in this publication meets the minimum requirements of American National Standard for Information Sciences Permanence of Paper for Printed Library Materials, ANSI/NISO Z39.48-1992.

Printed in the United States of America

To all the men and women of the Ipswich Public Schools who, when presented with the challenge of improving their schools over and above delivering each day's education, did not run from it, but like first responders ran toward the challenge. They consistently put what is best for students above all other considerations and worked tirelessly on behalf of those students.

Contents

Preface

Let's begin with a brief aside about our title. What do we mean by a "great school"? What we do *not* mean is a "perfect" school; nor do we mean the "greatest" school. We doubt there is a perfect school. While there certainly are wonderful schools, we don't believe that teachers and students at those schools would say they are perfect. Our title is not meant as any type of comparative assessment; instead, we favor individual school excellence.

It has been said (attributed to Theodore Roosevelt) that "comparison is the thief of joy," because comparison is open-ended in its ability to dwarf and thereby belittle all the good we are doing. No, to us a school is "great" if people love working there, are experiencing the joy of group accomplishment, and are achieving really good things for and with their students—achievements that are supported by data. The graduates themselves are the cumulative achievement of the school team. If we as a staff objectively believe that we have done an outstanding job for our graduates, then ours is a "great school." If we hold high standards, this is not an easy task.

With that explained, let's go on now to the story of our book.

The three of us worked together in the Ipswich, Massachusetts, public schools for fourteen years developing a unique "process" for improving schools based on quality management concepts and collaborative leadership skills. (We call it a process because unlike a program it has no conclusion; there is always something to improve or renew in a living entity like a school.)

When we began we were intent on answering three questions:

1. Could the principles of total quality management, which transformed many organizations in business and industry, be adapted successfully by public schools?

2. Could a system of collaborative leadership be devised that gave teachers a far more meaningful role in shaping the future of their school, while maintaining a clear chain of command and smoothly running daily operations?

3. Could a school transform its educational systems step by step from the inside out without any unusual infusion of funds, overhaul of staff, privatizing, or other wholesale disruption?

The answer to all three questions turned out to be a resounding YES!

The process produced results beyond what we might have imagined. The Ipswich School District began to be regarded as the equal of richer, more prestigious school districts, despite a per-pupil budget in the bottom third of school districts in Massachusetts. The Doyon School, where Ken was principal, went from the thirty-eighth percentile in state standardized testing to the ninety-second percentile. Curriculum and culture were vastly improved; teamwork was both productive and enjoyable, and faculty, staff, student, and parent morale were in the stratosphere.

Ken describes the outcome of using this collaborative process in his school:

"Energy kept flooding back at me. I kept wondering when the other shoe would drop. Would the process fall apart or run out of steam? It never did! Year after year we kept working together and good results piled upon good results. Step by step we transformed the culture and the curriculum. This happened because the collaborative process cultivated the continual renewal of motivation, teamwork, and ongoing cycles of focused goal accomplishment. We became a school that was "in the habit" of making improvements.

I could never have required staff to contribute the amount of energy they were expending. I wouldn't even have considered asking them to do all that they were doing. We wondered about this—what had happened inside of them? You could say that the process tapped into reservoirs of discretionary energy—and it did—but it was more than that. To call it intrinsic motivation is true, but an insufficient description; it was more profound than that.

We believe that these outcomes were possible because the staff trusted and believed in our collaboration being open, honest, and having admirable intentions; this allowed them to release their protective boundaries. The lines between the person and the work blurred. It spoke to their values—that their ideas were important, that they truly could make a difference. The process made it safe for them to risk aligning their deepest motivations with the future of the school."

They did something immensely valuable and it made them feel worthwhile. They were living the ideals that had brought them into education in the first place.

Mihaly Czikszentmihalyi's classic work *Flow: The Psychology of Optimal Experience* explores this condition, in which people achieve a state where inner satisfaction and productive work come together.

We are convinced that this same process can be transformational for a vast array of schools because it

- creates a vibrant, supportive atmosphere in the school among leadership, faculty, staff, and parents;
- provides teachers a far more meaningful and motivating role in planning for the future of the school;
- unites the school around a mutually created vision and an enthusiastically supported series of focused goals and objectives; and
- builds self-renewing "cycles of success," which over time transform the school's educational systems.

Let's take a brief advance look at three dynamics that make the process work. First, in order to excel, an organization needs to be *highly motivated*. The latest scientific trends show that the most powerful kind of motivation is intrinsic motivation. Not extrinsic carrot-and-stick motivation, but motivation that emanates from deep inside each person. Daniel Pink describes this type of motivation well in his best-selling book, *Drive*. When a school's workforce assumes ownership of the school's problems—and especially of its plans to improve—motivation and discretionary effort "go viral."

The collaborative leadership process, as we designed it, produces widespread ownership and intrinsic motivation. It empowers because real decision-making authority is shared—especially with the faculty.

The next factor to consider is whether the staff knows *how to work together* smoothly and productively. If the staff is able to work together as an efficient team, they can tackle goals and make substantial progress. This level of teamwork is easy to talk about, but difficult to obtain. Instilling motivation and inculcating outstanding teamwork doesn't just happen by itself. It is not the "default" state of affairs. Very few leaders are "naturals" at creating a highly motivated culture that excels at teamwork—leadership of that sort is an attainable skill that, like any other, requires the acquisition of concepts and tools.

Keeping in mind that changing an organization's culture and work patterns means changing how people think and interact, we incorporated into our leadership process all of the elements essential for facilitating and promoting the changes necessary for outstanding teamwork. Alan Deutschman articulately describes these elements in his book *Change or Die*. He observes that "facts, fear, and force" fail to change most people. He shows conclusively that, for the most part, even heart patients facing death, inmates on probation, or automobile workers facing the closing of their plant and loss of their jobs—absent other crucial elements of change—do not change long-term behavior despite what we would think of as the greatest motivation to do so.

According to Deutschman, the necessary elements of positive change are (a) a process based on hope, relationships, and mentoring, (b) a step-by-step articulated plan to move forward, and (c) multiple reinforcing experiences to maximize the likelihood that new behaviors will take root as new habits. The process we detail in the pages that follow contains clear steps to enable you to establish these indispensable elements in your organization.

Third is the issue of whether the school's improvement efforts will be steadfastly propelled forward by a *focused and mutually shared vision*, or, as is the unfortunate case for many schools, continually tossed this way and that by a confusing compendium of pendulum-swinging top-down edicts, reactions to events, and ever-changing searches for "silver bullets." Even the most well-intentioned plans will come to naught if the latter is the case. Change takes time, and *effective* change requires sticking with a well-designed process over an extended duration. It took ten years to fully transform the Doyon School. (Don't let that scare you, because it was highly rewarding and enjoyable all along the way.)

In her book entitled *Train Your Mind Change Your Brain*, *New York Times* writer Sharon Begley reports the results from numerous scientific experiments that explain aspects of how the brain functions. Several of those studies demonstrate that without the fixed attention of the subject, a performed activity is not likely to change the brain's neural patterns (i.e., if we are not focused, nothing happens in our brain).

Transposing that concept into the realm of seeking positive change in a school, we recognized that bringing a vision to life in a school would necessitate collaboratively prioritizing and focusing on no more than a few major goals at a time in order to unify and move the group forward with high energy. To make a vision come alive there is a need to nurture a sense of group consciousness in support of envisioned outcomes. To that end, we created a one-page school improvement plan that adds clarity, cohesiveness, and awareness to the vision. A mutually held and actively pursued vision and a set of sequential goals and objectives releases and focuses the school's energy.

Quality management techniques have worked for a diverse collection of leaders and organizations. There is a presumption in our book that the process we describe is replicable—that it isn't just a singular success by a unique leader or school district.

One basis for making this presumption is our own experience. Ken had been principal of the Doyon School for eight years when introduced to collaborative leadership and quality management concepts by Nels and Joe. From that time on he became an increasingly skilled, innovative practitioner of collaboration. He took command of the concepts. The difference in results between his first eight years and his last fourteen years was striking. His experience is a powerful testimony that the process can readily work for others. You too can take command of these same concepts.

Ken: "I had been Principal of the Doyon School for eight years. I would often stumble out of the end of a school year (or a school day!) as if I had been in a battle. There was no compelling professional reason for me to stay any longer. If lack of satisfaction as a school administrator was inevitable, I figured I might as well feel frustrated while earning more money.

"I had already been a finalist for assistant superintendent positions when I began working with Joe and Nels. As I saw what started to happen in my school, I withdrew all applications. I wanted to stay around and watch the growth of the seeds we were planting; it was fascinating to observe the impact of the collaborative energies, and too rewarding not to be a part of it. The process and the results were gratifying to me both professionally and personally. It became a joy to work within the culture this process created."

We consciously set out to adapt successful twenty-first-century leadership techniques to a school environment in a way that could be replicated by a principal and faculty in a typical school. We selected from among cutting-edge management principles those we saw as most helpful and adaptable to a school environment. Other elements and techniques were added from other sources and some we developed on our own. Teams of administrators and teachers worked with us and contributed their creative thinking to help us amend and employ the concepts.

We believe school leaders everywhere will benefit from an exploration of the philosophies underlying our collaborative leadership process, an examination of the various techniques that make those philosophies come alive, and the stories of our personal experiences regarding what it took to make it all work.

Our hearts and our hopes are connected to the strengthening of America's schools, and we see the ideas contained herein as essential for their revitalization. We wish to add some valuable tools to the leadership toolboxes of school boards and superintendents, principals, assistant principals, teacher leaders, central office supervisors, state and federal officials, and parents who care about the quality of their child's school. You are our indispensable readers. We are also hoping that colleges and universities with administrator certification programs or schools of education will include this book's thoughts about the transformative power of collaborative leadership in their curricula. The ultimate beneficiaries in all cases will be students.

If we can help leaders at the operational level of school management to employ a system of leadership that realizes the educational potential of their school, we will have achieved our purpose in writing this book.

HOW TO USE THE BOOK

We are big believers in concepts. As you read you will see that we have interwoven concepts from total quality management principles, twenty-first-century leadership skills, brain-based learning, social and emotional learning, teamwork and negotiating skills, and our own long and varied experiences. We then modified and assembled those concepts into a unique mosaic for use in an educational setting.

The preface, introduction, and first three chapters are focused on introducing these concepts. Don't seek to memorize anything, just begin to formulate a "helicopter view" of the larger background of ideas. After you become well grounded in the conceptual basis, you can then amend, extrapolate, and use these concepts creatively to fit your own specific circumstances.

Given that the process is ultimately built on relationships, we characterize it as more of an art form superimposed on a background of science. It can't be taught by asking you to follow the numbers. That disclaimer aside, chapters 4–6 take you through the process in detail (four "phases" containing a total of thirty-seven steps). Again, we expect you to skip or amend steps as is necessary; their purpose is to provide a guide so that you will not omit anything that might be essential for success. Even in these step-by-step chapters, great emphasis is placed on "mindset" (i.e., important thoughts to prepare you for a phase or step, or dynamics to be thinking about while the activity is taking place). We want you to know what to be watching for (and watching *out* for) so that the process will go well.

We suggest that you read the entire book once through to obtain a feel for and an overview of the concepts and process. When you are ready to proceed, you can return to chapter 4 and begin looking in detail at the step-by-step implementation. Key concepts have been italicized within the chapters and listed at the end of each chapter for emphasis and easy review.

Introduction

All parents hope to see their child attend a "great" school. Yet not all children, obviously, can attend the limited number of schools that are perceived as "superior." This was well depicted in the video documentary and book entitled *Waiting for Superman*, with children's lives seen as hanging in the balance on the hope of getting into that one special school. *The real challenge for education is to figure out how to turn a typical school into an extraordinary one.*

WHAT HAPPENED TO US CAN HAPPEN TO YOU

A group of people working together smoothly and effectively as a team, with high mutual respect, clear focus, and producing powerful results, is not the normal state of things. Someone has to put a process in place that enables this abnormal result to occur. That "someone" can be you.

We're pragmatic people; we wouldn't be taking the time to write this book unless we deeply believed (a) that the concepts presented herein have the power to *transform*, and (b) that what we experienced can and will happen in your school. We're sure that when you grasp the concepts at the center of our process, you will be able to adapt them with outstanding results in your particular circumstances.

We believe too that the process described herein provides school administration and teachers' associations a unique nonadversarial path forward—a path built on collaborative accomplishment, not conflict.

Ken: "The 2008 MCAS (Massachusetts Comprehensive Assessment System) data showed the Doyon School in the top 7 percent of Massachusetts elementary schools in grade four reading with 79 percent of students scoring either 'advanced' or 'proficient' and no students in the 'warning' category. These scores were a vast improvement from where we had been.

"At the same grade level, for example, in the 1999–2000 MCAS reading test, we fell below the state average, with only 15 percent of students scoring in the top two categories and a whopping 85 percent of students either in the categories of 'needs improvement' or 'warning.' When we started developing the school's collaborative improvement process, reaching even the 50th percentile in MCAS testing was seen as a very ambitious goal for our school. Little did we know at that time how far the process would take us.

"Test results were only one of the outcomes. Less easily measured but just as noteworthy were dramatic changes in faculty enthusiasm, teamwork and creative energies, increased student motivation to learn, and increased parent and community involvement and support. In fact, and based on survey as well as anecdotal data, we arrived at that most elusive of goals: a school that was in the habit of improvement—a school where it was a pleasure to come to work in the morning. This book explores in detail the concepts and activities that caused such dramatic improvements to occur."

THE HISTORICAL CONTEXT OF OUR IMPROVEMENT PROCESS

The ideological foundation for our partnership began when Nels Gustafson acquired the concepts of "Total Quality Management" (TQM) during his tenure as Human Resources Director at the Sylvania Corporation. Nels orchestrated the integration of quality principles into the management and operations of that 5,000-employee company.

When Nels left Sylvania, he began working with Joe Salah on an original approach that would apply TQM concepts and other leadership skills to public schools. Ken Cooper, a school principal with a deep knowledge of the practical workings of schools, joined Nels and Joe in refining the process; he began working with his staff at the Doyon School to shape and bring this unique improvement system to life over the course of more than a decade.

Why were we trying to bring TQM principles into a school? *TQM reconsiders organizations from the perspective of maximizing both productivity and job satisfaction.* It is a system for harnessing the intrinsic motivation of administration and staff, and constructing ongoing cycles of incremental improvement that over time transform an organization. In schools this means positively impacting student achievement as well as climate and culture.

THE ORIGINS OF TQM

After World War II, industry in the United States was leading the world and "sitting pretty"; meanwhile, Japanese industry, with its infrastructure heavily damaged, was trying to recover. Japan was producing inferior products with zero impact on international trade. In the late 1940s, a statistical analyst, W. Edwards Deming, and an engineer, Joseph Juran, were invited by the Japanese Union of Scientists and Engineers (JUSE) to come to Japan to share their innovative ideas about ways industries could consistently produce higher quality goods and services.

Deming and Juran were looking for a friendly ear, having failed to get a hearing from American industrial leaders. To make a long story short, they succeeded wildly. Toyota, one of the companies that adopted their methodologies, went from making *terrible* cars to eventually challenging the American industrial colossus General Motors. Many Japanese electronics companies like Sony became world leaders in their field. The quality management movement eventually found its way back to America, helping reinvent and renew companies like Ford, Motorola, Hewlett-Packard, and many others.

Below are Deming's famous fourteen principles of a quality management system (in our words).

1. Create constancy of purpose for improvement of products and service.
2. Adopt a new philosophy; become a learning organization.
3. Cease dependence on mass inspection; build quality into the product.
4. End awarding supplier contracts based only on price; make suppliers partners.
5. Work constantly to improve the system of production and service. Eliminate steps that are redundant or do not add value.
6. See that workers are properly trained; poor training often accounts for work failure.
7. Provide leadership focused on helping people to do a better job.
8. Drive fear out of the workplace; invite employees to ask questions and offer improvement ideas. Use systems thinking.
9. Break down barriers between various parts of the organization.
10. Eliminate slogans, exhortations, and numerical targets from the top; instead, collaboratively design improvement goals.
11. Eliminate quotas or work standards; emphasize quality production instead.
12. Find and eliminate barriers to pride in workmanship.
13. Institute a vigorous program of acquiring new knowledge and techniques.
14. Use teamwork and collaborative planning to transform productivity.

When we began working together in the 1990s, these fundamental TQM concepts had already been proven successful on the world stage with its biggest players as a way to produce great results in an organization. Our challenge was to determine whether the concepts could be successfully implemented in an average public school. Could we streamline them as to make it practicable for schools? Could we invent and integrate some new tools to promote teamwork and focused goal setting in a manner that would fit within a typical school's system of operations?

Would these processes be accepted by teachers and teacher associations? Could they be applied systematically and successfully without creating controversy and disruption in a public institution with so many stakeholders? Would a typical staff, perhaps weary or skeptical from frequent program changes, get past looking upon the effort as just another "*program du jour*"—here today gone tomorrow—and invest their energies? Would everyone stick with it long enough for the results to accumulate and make a long-term difference? Fortunately, the answer to all questions was "YES."

APPLYING TQM TO A TYPICAL SCHOOL

Our adaptation of TQM concepts focused on producing four key outcomes:

- Teamwork, getting everyone working together;
- Ownership of the school's future by all key constituencies, uniting the school community behind a mutually created vision and focused "high-motivation" goals;
- Collaborative systems thinking, working together to transform the school's educational systems piece-by-piece, step-by-step; and
- Continuous improvement, sticking with it to amass success upon success over a period of years.

TQM principles are not "instant pudding"; it takes years to truly transform any organization. Changing organizations means changing *people*, especially in the way they approach their work.

Looking carefully at the four bulleted elements above, ask yourself whether any school can make meaningful improvement without them. Each of these elements is essential to achieving long-term transformation in a school or any organization, but there is no silver bullet or shortcut to obtain them. They do not happen by wishing or by good intentions or by accident—a well-designed process is needed and must be faithfully applied.

So why is TQM less of a hot-button item today? We agree with the prescient observations of Mike Schmoker and Richard Wilson in their article, "Transforming Schools through Total Quality Education" (AASA 1994). They noted that some schools and organizations were adopting the trappings of quality management without transferring any real power or trust to employees. We'd add that when TQM was in vogue, too many treated it like "instant pudding or a silver bullet."

We focused on its essential qualities, like teamwork, power sharing, goal focusing, systems thinking, and continuous improvement—and then gave it the time it needs. The truth is that these essentials are as relevant and have the same power to transform today as when Deming and Juran introduced them to the world.

Our book provides the details of how such a process of change, focused on essentials, was adapted to schools—a process that we carefully describe herein to enable school leaders anywhere to experience the same transformational effect on their school.

FULFILLING LEADERSHIP VISIONS

Ken: "When beginning our careers as principals, we typically hope to have an energizing and unifying impact on our school. We picture ourselves working alongside a motivated faculty while focusing on improving curriculum and instruction for the benefit of our students.

"The catch is that becoming that kind of collaborative leader may be fine to aspire to in the abstract, but it is much more difficult to realize when you are in the 'trenches' being assaulted by the stress of daily events. Our goal is to supply both the knowledge and the practical skills to assist school leaders in becoming the inspired leader they envisioned when choosing to become a school administrator. That is what happened to me! In fact, what happened to me far surpassed the dreams I had when I first became a school principal."

It took much of what we learned in our ninety combined years of diverse work experiences—Ken in education, Nels in human resources and quality management, Joe in the military, local government, and business—to put together the contents of this book. *While it took many years to obtain the experience to write this book, ours is not an "old" book. Make no mistake, while built on the best of the past, this book is about leadership in the twenty-first century.*

Our work focuses on changes in leadership style necessary to successfully lead today's workforce; that's where we begin in chapter 1. We offer a more productive alternative to top-down leadership, which intrinsically and inevitably creates conflict and discord between management and employees who wish to be empowered, wastes precious time in contentiousness that would be better spent on improvement, and fails to fully utilize employees' abilities.

The ideas and experiences contained herein will help any organization where good teamwork is desired and high achievement is hoped for.

Ken: "As I recollect, but would not have understood at the time, I had been moving on a track through positions and schools without ever having a deep and profound effect on the school I was a part of. It wasn't from lack of caring or hard work or even ability, because I contributed caring, hard work, and the best of my abilities to each position. It was because there were some aspects of leadership and systems thinking that I did not yet understand.

"What I learned about organizational leadership over the past seventeen years made a world of difference for my school, and what I learned about human behavior changed who I am—it made me a better person. We discuss these transforming concepts in the context of a school, but the fact is they are the same for any organization; just change the word school to running an office, little league, charity, or small business. The principles are the same: Fear is fear, trust is trust, motivation is motivation, and moving forward together is the same thing whatever the context."

Nels and Joe: "We have great respect for the amount of effort and dedication it takes for a school's staff to handle the overwhelming number of problems brought to them each day by their hundreds of students—much less for them to also embark on a substantive improvement process. When you are completely absorbed and fatigued by keeping your ship running and afloat, it takes brave souls to simultaneously take on the task of a wholesale renovation of the ship. Schools have a lot of brave souls manning the ship.

"We were most fortunate to run into Ken Cooper. If you drop a good idea anywhere near him, he will pick it up and run with it to places you never imagined. There are other terrific leaders in the Ipswich public schools who have also embraced and applied many of the concepts you will find in this book. Through the efforts of these leaders and their selfless, dedicated staffs, their school district has achieved exceptional results."

WHAT'S IN THE BOOK?

This book is organized into six chapters. Chapters 1–3 are meant to provide a clear understanding of the concepts behind our process. The concluding three chapters (4–6) offer a step-by-step guide for putting the process in place. The appendixes contain handouts, training materials, and sample surveys.

On your journey through the book you'll be provided with

- how to transition conceptually from old top-down dictates to a more productive twenty-first-century leadership style;
- methods of fostering and harnessing enthusiasm and intrinsic motivation;
- numerous practical suggestions to enhance the credibility and effectiveness of school leadership;
- strategies to inspire outstanding and enjoyable teamwork;
- a set of working values that will elevate your working culture;
- a guide to "consensus" decision making;

- a model for running effective meetings;
- proven models for planning and problem solving;
- approaches to help unite staff behind a set of common goals;
- a sequence of steps that will powerfully focus the energies of your staff behind a shared vision and a prioritized set of goals and objectives;
- techniques to anticipate and overcome roadblocks and deadlocks; and
- a system for self-renewal that will produce ongoing cycles of success.

Chapter One

The Need for a Different Kind of Leadership

OPERATING BY AN OLD PARADIGM IN A NEW WORLD

When recruiting building principals, it is common for districts to promote classroom teachers who have received administrator training, experience, and certification. Once they have assumed their new positions, they are presented with various mandates from the district level, and it is assumed that they will promulgate policies with everyone in the school in support.

There is an unspoken assumption that teachers and staff are just waiting to comply enthusiastically with initiatives from the school committee, superintendent of schools, or their principal. Not that anyone actually says, "Oh, yes, they are just waiting for us to tell them what to do." Nobody says that, but many in education act as if this notion were true by giving top-down orders and expecting to see great results.

We can only lead by methodologies that we know. All of our lives we've observed leaders giving orders and have been led to believe that that is leadership. That *was* leadership—leadership for employees of the past.

Employees today will comply with directives from above to the degree that they must do so to keep their jobs. But today's employees will not act with enthusiasm or dig into discretionary reservoirs of creativity and energy as a group, unless they believe in and have a sense of ownership of what they are doing.

In his book *Bringing Out the Best in People*, Dr. Aubrey Daniels reports that on surveys (with sample sizes as large as 10,000 persons), when asked, the majority of workers consistently agreed that they could do more on the job if they were inspired to do so. Those who answered "Yes" were then asked, "How much more?" The numbers were significant, with most re-

1

sponses falling within the 30–40 percent range of additional creativity and energy that could be given. Respondents who estimated their additional available energy to be above that range, some as high as 67 percent, qualified their response by noting that it was true only if they worked in a system that was not "competency-suppressing."

Since school leaders rely upon faculty and staff to produce educational excellence in their school, the key question becomes: "What can school leaders do to enable faculty and staff to become highly motivated partners in the task of making their school the best possible school?" This is the most fundamental of "need to know" questions for administrators. "How can I maximize the collective impact of the people in my school?"

The form of leadership carried over from the ages of hierarchy—patriarchal, top-down, order-giving—is for the most part dead today—dead, that is, as a means to obtain the best performance from an organization. *It is, however, not a death that is yet widely recognized.* The top-down system is still in extensive use. The old way was for someone to be put in charge, let that person tell us what to do, and then we, the supporting cast, would take action based on our trained sense of duty and obligation. We saw that system working in the 1940s, 1950s, and early 1960s.

Then something began to change. In America, we've always had a skeptical view of hierarchy based on national characteristics such as a history with no royalty; no formalized class structure; a governing system based on one-person/one-vote; independently run states, cities, and towns; and a Constitution built on the concept that "all men are created equal." While these factors are the basis of our governmental principles, a hierarchical system of leadership, brought from our nations of origin, nevertheless became well entrenched in the running of many of our organizations.

This top-down, chain of command system goes back to kings, queens, and military organizations of old. Because many have experienced no other method of leadership, they understand and use it. This is our past. It is time to transition to our future—a future that will be not only more productive but more in harmony with our beliefs.

In the past fifty years, social and economic trends have tipped the scales heavily toward a sense of individual empowerment. Consider, for example, the five following trends. First, everywhere we turn, we are deluged by an endless stream of commercials transmitting the unspoken message that each of us is important since all the major businesses of our society are spending multi-billions of dollars to obtain our individual support. Reinforcing the sense that each of us *matters* is the feedback/customer satisfaction surveys that we are increasingly being asked to complete following transactions.

Second, there has been a strong legal trend emphasizing defendant and consumer rights. We have seen the resulting explosion in the number of lawsuits seeking to protect and further the rights of individuals.

Third, we have taken the 1960s dictum to heart to "question authority." In movies and television it has become commonplace for the villain to be an authority figure, someone who in the past would have been looked up to. Recent legislation has been passed in many jurisdictions protecting the rights of "whistle-blowers," encouraging individuals to speak up when they believe those in authority have committed a wrong.

Fourth, higher education has moved into the mainstream of the population. In his contribution to the excellent anthology *Quality Goes to School* (AASA 1994), Peter Drucker credits World War II's GI Bill of Rights as "signaling the shift to a knowledge society." Leaders used to have the distinct advantage of being more educated than those whom they supervised; this is no longer true. It is becoming commonplace to have college graduates in families at every economic level.

Fifth is the empowerment made possible by the rapid advance of technology and information. The proliferation of information coming through the Internet largely erases the advantages those in the hierarchy had when they alone had access to specialized information in their field. Each of us can carry in our pocket access to encyclopedic knowledge via smartphones. Moreover, we have "apps" to tell us the weather, where to get the cheapest gas, and how to navigate to a particular location. We can listen to just the music we want to hear when we want to hear it, and if we want to watch a movie or television program we can watch it "on demand." Is this empowering? Absolutely.

Leaders today are leading a very different work force; people are motivated by what *they* see as important, not by what others tell them is important—from the latter, the typical response you can expect is compliance, as opposed to enthusiastic and energized follow-through.

These factors, and others, have altered the playing field for leaders. There has been a great shift in attitude against *complying enthusiastically* merely because we receive orders from above. *However, that doesn't mean that employees today are unwilling to truly invest themselves in their work.* There are numerous examples today of organizations where employees are so engaged by teamwork and a participatory process that they function at the highest levels of motivation and creativity.

People have great qualities to contribute. Virtually all workers want the organizations they work for to be successful; and they want a sense of contributing to that success. They want to feel good about what they are doing in their work life. Given the changes in our society, it's going to take a different style of leadership to bring these qualities to the surface.

A NEW KIND OF LEADERSHIP

Truly charismatic leaders can inspire their workforce to comply with enthusiasm. They are master salespersons. People buy what they are selling. They have a presence that gives weight to what they say and a charisma that people respond to. The problem is that there are many organizations in need of excellent leadership but the Winston Churchills and John F. Kennedys of the world are rare.

While there are few who are able to inspire uniquely, there are many of us in leadership positions in need of a way to obtain the same powerful results. While we don't know of any way to "learn" to become a charismatic leader, the techniques of becoming a collaborative leader *can* be learned and *are* attainable.

Ken: "Before I began to use this collaborative process, I felt like the lines of a giant net were slung over my shoulder. In the net were my faculty, staff, parents, and students. It was a tremendous, wearying, debilitating struggle to try to pull that net along. As I implemented the collaborative leadership process, my faculty and staff came abreast of me and at times moved ahead! Parents too became engaged and were highly supportive.

"*My first big step toward becoming a collaborative leader was to learn to 'trust the group.'* The problem was I didn't know how to do that. Such letting go was outside of my experience and I was afraid of appearing to be a weak leader.

"Joe and Nels emphasized that the group (my faculty and stakeholders) wouldn't always think as I did, but they *would* tackle meaningful issues and, if the process were fair, open, and well run, they would make good decisions. In addition, because of their sense of ownership, they would get a great deal done. It wasn't easy at first for me to trust in this way. However, as we went along, and as the positive results piled up, it became second nature for me to usher emerging topics and issues through the group process. I began to note and appreciate how the group shaped and improved ideas, how they identified and discarded less-promising suggestions, how they helped us avoid potentially costly mistakes, and how they got behind the plans that we made."

Nels: "When I was director of human resources, Sylvania's general manager put me in charge of overseeing its quality management initiative. We had over 5,000 employees all across the country. As a part of that initiative, we provided a lot of supervisor training. Most supervisors were used to the old style of leadership: Kick butt and push a lot of product out the door. It was very hard for some of them to adapt to a style that involved more collaboration and teamwork with their employees, but they did amazingly well once they embraced the concepts. Sure there were still times when a supervisor had to hold people firmly to performance standards; but these times no longer defined their unit's culture.

"For the old-fashioned, 'I'm-in-control, butt-kicking' supervisor, making this discovery was a real eye-opener: *Not only does collaboration make it more enjoyable to come to work each day; it is also more productive—it puts more high quality work out the door.*"

There are many facets to this new empowering kind of leadership. Let's begin by examining three key qualities. A twenty-first-century school leader needs to be *a collaborative leader, a culture creator*, and *a process leader.*

A COLLABORATIVE LEADER

There are five ways for a leader to make a decision: (1) alone, (2) with informal input, (3) with comprehensive, carefully considered input, (4) in consensus partnership with others, and (5) by delegating the decision to others. We recommend using (1) and (2) for routine administration, (3) for important decisions within regular operations, (4) for school improvement planning, and (5) for subtasks prior to decision making. In this way, regular operations have a clear chain of command and run smoothly, while the most important decisions about the future are made collaboratively.

An important line of reasoning regarding collaboration goes like this: *If you need others to successful implement a goal or objective* you have two choices: (1) make the decision and then try to sell it to everyone, or (2) involve all who are needed to implement the decision in prior discussions and planning. This latter approach produces far better results by engaging those who are needed for implementation in a manner that increases the likelihood that they will care about making it a success.

If you have any doubts about our conclusion, just ask whether you yourself would value the opportunity to participate in decisions that impact your work. Consider also how *disrespectful* it is for decisions to be made without hearing from those who have intimate knowledge of the factors involved in the decision, and whose performance and working conditions will affect the outcome.

It is quick and easy to make decisions by yourself or with a small group. Obtaining enthusiastic implementation of those decisions across the whole organization is another matter altogether. Success is not inextricably tied to making decisions most quickly; it is, however, dependent upon obtaining enthusiastic implementation of widely supported decisions.

A CULTURE CREATOR

The people who work in a school or in any organization have collectively within them enormous reservoirs of knowledge, ability, energy, and creativity. Although many people regard leadership as a matter of *control*, the most important job of a leader is actually to *release* the organization's energy, because that energy has the greatest positive effect on the organization's accomplishments.

As a culture creator, the leader's focus is on helping his or her staff to grow both in competence and motivation to the point where they need minimal supervision—just occasional support, feedback, and kudos. The influence of the leader is then highly leveraged through the time and effort of many others in their workforce who are on the same page. Compare this to controlling leaders under whom system advances can be made only with their initiation, permission, and guidance.

It is our experience that the old-fashioned, top-down way of leading is so stifling and narrow in scope that results do not compare to a system that multiplies motivation throughout the organization. The collaborative leader's influence and impact on the organization is substantially increased, though the leader may get less direct credit for improvements. As the Chinese philosopher Lao Tzu noted, a leader is truly great when his or her people achieve the desired goal and then say, "We did it ourselves."

For a self-motivated, self-renewing, highly enthusiastic culture to emerge, the leader must focus on

- establishing a comprehensive and clearly communicated step-by-step process for moving forward;
- improving the staff's interpersonal skills;
- providing language and opportunities for effective and open communication;
- signaling that improvement is a priority by allotting it scheduled time;
- instilling a sense of ownership in the workforce by sharing school improvement planning decisions;
- setting high expectations;
- keeping efforts focused on just a few goals at any one time;
- being transparent and unbiased;
- building trust and reducing fear;
- helping the group through bottlenecks;
- resolving disputes before they spread;
- inspiring and setting the example;
- reaching out to the knowledge base of the staff;
- allowing for experimentation and healthy risk-taking;
- creatively measuring and celebrating the organization's effort and growth;

- steadfastly concentrating the organization's resources and efforts on improvement priorities; and
- keeping the process fresh and alive by renewing it each year.

By these methods, it is not charisma that engages people; instead, they become caught up in the enjoyment and sense of accomplishment that comes from successfully working together toward a shared vision. They become inspired by the most powerful form of motivation—their own intrinsic motivation.

School superintendent Rick Korb says this about the culture created in the Ipswich schools: "Our culture is the glue that holds us together and allows us to achieve. It defines us as an educational family working toward collaborative goals in a supportive atmosphere. We are able to proactively address issues before they become problems because people listen to each other. In my years here, I have quite amazingly had only one grievance that went past an initial resolution." Ken adds to this, even more amazingly, that he did not have a single grievance filed at the Doyon School in the fourteen years after the collaborative school improvement process was put into place.

A PROCESS LEADER

As a process leader you are not thinking up solutions and selling them. You are no longer Mr. or Ms. Fix Everything. You are not substituting your judgment for the judgment of others. That is the old way. Where to focus improvement efforts and how to accomplish improvements are decided by consensus decision making with your faculty, staff, parents, and school council if you have one. You no longer need to have all the answers. Your job is to lead the group through a series of process steps and to focus on achieving the next process step (i.e., to keep the group moving forward). Over time these incremental steps will transform your school.

As a process leader you become concerned with

- allocating sufficient time for improvement;
- focusing your workforce on identifying and prioritizing improvement goals;
- ensuring that chosen goals reflect what is best for students;
- helping the group generate specific objectives and action plans for each targeted goal;
- providing resources to support each goal;
- monitoring and supporting effective plan implementation; and
- renewing and refreshing the process each year.

Rather than focusing on how to sell their own priorities for improvement, process leaders focus on powerfully building the improvement system and keeping that system moving until it transforms their school or organization.

You may be thinking that this doesn't seem like leadership at all. It certainly is. This leadership is inclusive and respectful of the contribution of others. This leadership establishes an atmosphere in which people grow and thrive. As they grow, many additional leaders will emerge and work hard to make the school a better place. You will have multiplied yourself and leveraged your effectiveness. This real and powerful form of leadership leads to accomplishments and achievements otherwise unobtainable.

If you genuinely mean what you say when you offer to share the power to improve your school with your staff, if you are sincere about keeping the process honest and open, if you do not break trust, and if you treat staff respectfully as intelligent, caring, creative professionals, you will succeed.

It is our job to help you understand the concepts necessary to become such a leader. We will also provide a step-by-step blueprint for establishing a *collaborative improvement process* in your school. If you are already a collaborative leader we hope to help you to further hone your skills.

We'll end this chapter by responding to a few "frequently asked questions."

DO I COLLABORATE ABOUT EVERYTHING?

Our process does not ask you to collaborate on the running of every aspect of the school. The scope of collaboration that we have designed is far narrower than that. It would call for a much too complex and specialized a management system to ask leaders to run all the operations of a school using collaborative decision making. That would not be a plan that a typical school could implement.

Our process calls for full collaboration and sharing decision-making power in one area: that of planning for ways to improve your school. Collaboration for school improvement is strategically important enough to foster a sense of ownership throughout the life of the school.

Once an improvement has been chosen, planned, and implemented, it becomes integrated into day-to-day operations and is then managed by the traditional chain of command. Day-to-day operations will never be exactly the same; more people will now want to pitch in to see that the planned changes go well. It is likely that you will use teams to plan and organize the implementation of certain changes. It is also likely that you will want to solicit the input of the staff before making operational decisions that affect working conditions and the curriculum.

However, the structure of day-to-day operations in our process remains organizationally traditional, the same as the one you are most familiar with now. The principal is the primary decision maker in daily operations while sharing decision-making power in the area of *planning for school improvement*. We will make this important distinction even clearer as we go along.

This innovation in design—collaboration within a powerful but limited scope that targets improvement planning—makes the process of collaborative teamwork accessible to all schools. We developed this system to carefully balance two important needs: the need for time-efficient and clear-cut daily decision making, with the need for widespread ownership and participation in creating a great future for the school.

IS COLLABORATIVE LEADERSHIP TOO SLOW FOR ME?

Correctly identifying what needs to happen next in your school as well as being right about how to make those improvements is unfortunately not enough—it doesn't mean that people will be supportive and follow you.

In her insightful best-selling book, *The Death and Life of the Great American School System*, Diane Ravitch tells the story of a disastrous attempt to implement "balanced literacy" in the San Diego, California, school district during the years 1998–2005. While many teachers conceptually supported the balanced-literacy program itself, they recoiled and resisted the top-down, boss-mandated, "do it or else," nature of the implementation.

The school board and the superintendent acknowledged quite openly that they felt there was "no time for collaboration or consensus." It was "their way or the highway." The climate of "fear and suspicion" that ensued lead to the replacement of 90 percent of the building principals, a turnover of more than a third of the teaching staff, sketchy implementation of the program, and only modest student gains (which were actually less than the improvement made by California schools statewide during the same period).

Dr. Jeffrey Cruikshank and Dr. Lawrence Susskind, in their book, *Breaking the Impasse*, give a name to what follows after making top-down backroom decisions. They call this sequence of events "*decide, announce, defend.*" Yes, one person or a small group can make a decision quickly; getting others to implement the decision is the problem. Because others do not understand all that has gone into the decision, because they predictably will have points of view that the decision makers did not take into consideration, or just because the idea is new—*fear is inevitably triggered.*

When fear is triggered, people become defensive and form groups with like-minded persons. These cliques then move to block or sabotage the proposed action or take it in a new direction. *By the time the in-fighting is all sorted out there is likely to be enough emotional damage and tactical confu-*

sion to make successful implementation impossible. Often in the course of these battles, the issue ends up back at square one, thus nurturing cynicism— a lot of sound and fury but little progress. Most of us have been part of such improvement initiatives that tire everyone out while at most making a minimum of progress. It won't be long before the search for the next "program of the month" is under way.

Fear is triggered when people think, "What are they going to do to me?" This is fear of the unknown. It would be highly unusual for fear to be generated when thinking, "What are we going to do to ourselves?" People don't fear *change* itself so much as they fear *being changed against their will.*

Think of fear this way: *fear equals dynamite.* Find out what people are worried about. Take fear out of the process as soon as you can. If you proceed with meetings without first discovering and defusing the dynamite, don't be surprised if there is an explosion. Collaboration allows worries to be put on the table early in a nonthreatening atmosphere. Instead of blowing up, such worries are dealt with successfully beforehand.

When people see themselves as valued participants, when their concerns—their fears—are addressed early in the process, they become free to focus on and embrace the positives of new ideas. This is even more likely when the group operates by true consensus because they know that any concerns they may have will be heard, considered, and ameliorated if possible.

Two helpful references regarding reducing fear are W. Edwards Deming's *Out of the Crisis* and *Driving Fear Out of the Workplace*, by Kathleen Ryan and Daniel Oestreich.

Our alternative to "decide, announce, defend," is to lead the group that is going to implement the decision through a process in which *they* come to understand and own the improvement initiative. It is likely they will then enthusiastically participate in bringing the vision to reality. At first glance it might appear that such a method takes longer, because collaboration and reaching consensus takes time. The fact is, in the end, it is a *shorter process.*

When asking the question: "Is collaboration too slow?" one needs to pay attention to what is being measured. *The most meaningful measure is the time it takes to get to enthusiastic implementation of a decision, as opposed to focusing on the time it takes to reach a decision.*

It is our experience that a collaborative process is more time-efficient because so many top-down decisions never arrive at enthusiastic implementation and never really make a difference; those few that do often arrive after an extended and debilitating period of misunderstanding, in-fighting, and damage control. Hard feelings are generated by the combative nature of this kind of decision-making process. These feelings will come back to haunt future improvement initiatives.

Dr. William Glasser, a psychiatrist who focused on working relationships (and who was a guest speaker at Ken's school), summed up the combative nature of top-down management (in his book *The Control Theory Manager*), by warning that workers who are "dominated" will spend *too much of their energy struggling to gain a sense of freedom*—energy that could be better spent in the pursuit of accomplishments.

WHAT IF THEY DON'T CHOOSE MY GOALS?

As a leader, you probably have a creative mind and a grasp of what is going on in your building. It is likely that you have in mind certain priorities for the school, and you want them to become a reality. What if you embark on a collaborative process and at the outset your staff and stakeholder groups pick goals that are not your top priority? This is a possible outcome, and it *is a perfectly good outcome*—here's why.

Your goal as a collaborative process leader is not to have your own specific ideas put into action. Your goal is to release the school's energy by building a thriving culture and an improvement process that over time will make the school a far better place than implementing any one person's ideas could ever have achieved. You are engaged in an improvement process that is bigger than your own ideas.

In the next chapter we present a set of "working values." One of them is entitled "Not My Ideas, But the Best Ideas." The process of identifying solutions that work is a search for the best ideas: To find the best ideas, *we need to be objective about all ideas including our own.*

When Ken led his staff through the process of determining his school's first set of teamwork goals, revising the reading program was the consensus choice of stakeholders as the place to begin—and it happens that this was also his top goal. What if it hadn't turned out that way? What if the group, through an open process, believed that somewhere else was a more important place to start? This is fine! The most important thing is that the group has engaged, has begun an ongoing process to improve their school together, and that *the process is being guided by what is best for students*. As long as the process is objective and guided by what is best for students, the group will choose worthwhile goals.

As process leader, you get to describe and recommend the improvement goals you favor as a participating member of the consensus group (which can vary, as we will explain later). Because you are sharing decision-making authority with the group in this area, because you are open and honest with them, they become very caring and responsive to your views. If the group does choose to start somewhere else, understand that over time they will surely get to your areas of concern. The criteria for decision making provided in later chapters make it highly probable that the consensus group will make wise decisions about where to begin.

At the start of the collaborative improvement process, building trust, unity, and motivation are more important than the issue of what potential improvements to take on first. We are not saying that which goal you start with is unimportant; it is important. We are saying that establishing a culture of trust and transparent consensus is more important at the start.

When your staff gets to the goals you personally see as most important, even if it doesn't happen immediately, they will arrive as an empowered team acting with enthusiasm and motivation. They will then make your goals come to life in a way that will exceed your hopes and most optimistic expectations.

HOW WILL EMBRACING COLLABORATION IMPACT MY CAREER?

School leaders are skilled, knowledgeable people. While most are not innately charismatic, they are fully capable of leading an inspired school, a school that uses everyone's abilities in a process of collaborative teamwork. Leaders today need to embrace a collaborative system to achieve the success that their communities, parents, students, and they themselves hope for—it's right for the times and will be embraced and appreciated by the people with whom you work.

If a collaborative approach to improvement is embraced at the district level, as was our fortunate case in Ipswich, the positive impact will be felt at the administrative level as well. For the first twelve years after Nels and Joe began to work with the Ipswich schools, no school principal left. Only retirements eventually broke up the district's leadership team.

This is a powerful indicator; teamwork and collaboration help school leaders feel good about the work they are doing and where they are working. Once they have been part of a collaborative system, they will not be anxious to move on and go back to a top-down system with all its politics and infighting. They will be understandably reluctant to move somewhere they would have to begin "all over again" in the hope of finding a culture that values them and provides the same opportunity for accomplishment.

Our experience also suggests that teachers similarly enjoy and remain at schools in which their contributions are respected and where they play an important role in planning for student achievement. A 2010 study in the North Carolina *Journal of School Choice* ("Empowerment, Leadership, and Teachers' Intentions to Stay or Leave") examined high rates of teacher attrition and migration in charter schools. The authors compiled numerous studies showing that shared decision making and leadership support were top reasons why a teacher would stay or leave.

Employee retention and continuity of leadership is crucial if school improvement is to build from year to year.

A REVIEW OF CHAPTER 1 CONCEPTS

- Top-down, boss management is an old paradigm in a new world.
- People today feel personally empowered; they no longer comply with enthusiasm merely because they are told to do so.
- Many organizations are in need of being run well; collaborative leadership provides every organization with the chance for outstanding leadership.
- A twenty-first-century school leader needs to be a collaborative leader, a culture creator, and a process leader.
- How long it takes to get to enthusiastic implementation is what we really ought to be measuring, not how long it takes to make a decision.
- Success is about obtaining enthusiastic implementation of widely supported decisions.
- In a collaborative system, people are inspired by their own intrinsic motivation.
- Limiting full collaboration to improvement planning makes it practical and accessible.
- Building trust, unity, and motivation are more important initially than which potential improvements to take on first.
- The leader helps the group discover and accomplish what they want to do together.
- The collaborative process is effective at defusing fear.
- As collaborative leaders grow the culture, they multiply and leverage their impact and influence on the organization.
- A thriving culture and a dynamic improvement process produces far more progress than implementing any one person's ideas.

Chapter Two

The Need for Outstanding Working Relationships

UPGRADING RELATIONSHIPS FIRST

To set and achieve goals productively, a staff must first be able to work together effectively. A school building and educational materials are inanimate objects without people to give them life. Isn't it logical, therefore, that if people bring the organization to life, the ability of those people to work well together becomes a—perhaps even *the*—key determining factor in an organization's ability to pursue improvement initiatives?

Some leaders think, "Work is work; we 'do' feelings at home, not here in the workplace." We ought not to pretend that personal characteristics like patience, understanding, tolerance, encouragement, and empathy don't play an important role in our work environment. The business of working together is far from all business. The point is made by the expression, "I thought I was hiring employees but got people instead." We all carry around the full range of human emotions—even at work. That being the case, people in the workplace need a common vision of how to successfully relate to one another in order to become free to concentrate on doing their best work. If they feel safe they can put the best of themselves into their work.

Achievement is built on positive working relationships. Relationships are built on trust. Our job as leaders is to strengthen working relationships by building trust—and reducing fear and conflict. Relational issues left unresolved will interfere with the accomplishment of school improvement goals.

Ken: "For most of the first year of implementing our collaborative improvement process at the Doyon School we concentrated on working relationships. I really felt there was something 'broken' in our personal interactions with one another and that was where we had to begin. I told Joe and

15

Nels, 'Before we talk about setting goals, we've got to deal with relation-ships among our staff.'

"We held a series of meetings over six months' time that focused on three sets of questions:

1. Why are you here? What brought you into education?
2. What do you need from the rest of the staff? What kind of support do we want to receive from one another?
3. What do we want from a set of working values? What should our working values do for us? What working values can we all agree upon?

The 'what brought us here' dialogue was an opportunity to get in touch with common positive values and motivations; it gave us the chance to see our similarities and admire the ideals held by our coworkers. We felt empathy and experienced a collective validation. Anything that reveals the best side of people to each other is constructive. It connects us through powerful positive emotions and contributes to formation of a shared vision.

"The questions concerning the 'kind of support we want from one an-other' broke open an emotional floodgate. At a certain point one teacher said to another, 'To see you dragging your ass down the hallway without even a hello to acknowledge anyone else is disheartening to me and is a depressing way to start the day. Teaching children should be a joy.' This kicked off a frank discussion of what was needed from each other—a discussion about how each of us has the power to help colleagues get through their day successfully, or conversely, to make it harder for them.

"Our meetings about working relationships changed everything! The new culture of our school began to be born. It became clear that in most cases, the life-choices that led us to teaching were based on motivations and values that we held in common. Individuals shared, sometimes with great emotion, how much working with children meant to them, and why it was such an impor-tant and rewarding part of their lives. This was as close to a *catharsis* as you are going to get in a faculty meeting. The transition we made was a huge leap forward, going from looking at one another guardedly to thinking, 'I am working with a very special group of people.'"

BLAME NO ONE; FIX THE PROBLEM

It is important to interject a note of caution regarding the dangers inherent in opening such candid conversations. Don't allow the group to become mired in blame or in the past. Draw the lessons from the past, then quickly transi-tion to a forward-looking posture.

Looking backward often becomes focused on blame. Groups are not united by looking backward; they unite by looking forward to solutions. Brain research shows us that when we are in a defensive frame of mind, in something we call "emotions-only mode," people will reject logic. That's why in heated arguments nobody ever changes their mind—until they calm down and use the reasoning part of their brain to compare ideas more objectively. Using a blame perspective ignites fear and sets off defense shields all across the meeting.

Here is an approach for looking back that minimizes the damage. Announce up front the desire to focus on the issues and not make comments personal. Avoid blame. Talk about issues, not people. We need to learn from experience, but not in a destructive way. As soon as we have identified the lesson from the past, it is important to turn the conversation forward by stating, "Now that we know what we don't want, let's talk about what we do want."

Some North American Indian tribes used a great method to resolve disputes that embraced the following approach. The parties to the dispute gathered in a meeting governed by these rules: "*Nothing can be said in the negative. Only talk in a positive way about what we want to see happen in the future.*" This changes how ideas are presented.

An issue that could have been presented in the negative, when a tribal member might have said, "So-and-so acted selfishly and used more than their fair share of our common store of necessities," is instead raised more forwardly and objectively when approached this way: "I want to ensure that everyone gets their fair share of the tribal stores and that there are no inequities." Both comments address the same issue, but in a very different way and with different results.

We can see that the first statement would set off a defensive argument because the thrust of the comment is to look back, personalize, and blame. After a harangue of conflicting points of view and differing reasons, perceptions, and rationalizations, if we are very lucky, the conversation *might* get around to discussing "how do we make things fair?" Since that is the way to resolution, why not go there straight away? It is a psychologically brilliant system. It allows all parties to agree on what a fair system is, knowing that they will never reach agreement about who is to blame and why.

The comment at Ken's meeting about a fellow teacher "dragging into school" could have had negative repercussions if taken the wrong way. In the early phase of a dialogue, take care when looking back at events that nothing is said that will make it harder to move forward.

PEOPLE ARE NOT AFRAID OF CHANGE

Early in the process, Ken told his faculty, "There are many routes to excellence and we need to find ours together. I will not substitute my vision for the collective wisdom of the group." A number of faculty members told him later that when he said that they started to lose their fear of the process. Why did they feel that way? Because if there are many possible routes to excellence and we are truly going to find ours together, then I don't have to be worried that this process is really all about the principal's preconceived plan to get what he or she wants.

Much of our experience in organizations has been with people trying to have us endorse and implement their plans. This makes us wary and "on the lookout" for those who are trying to control the process.

Because people are wary of being hurt by proposed change, we think they are afraid of change. People are not afraid of change. They are afraid of being hurt.

People are afraid of expending effort toward a result that never happens—of exposing themselves by caring and then being bitterly disappointed—and worse, of being used. They are afraid of being trapped in uncomfortable positions as a result of changed policies. They are afraid they will no longer be able to do some things that they value and enjoy. They are afraid of being forced out of their comfort zones and wary of what the process will ask of them. Change raises the specter of these results, and since it is difficult to structure a change process in a manner in which people will relax and participate without fear, it appears that people are afraid of change.

To the contrary, they all—everyone, even the most diehard "you-can't-do-its"—would like to be a part of a process in which their organization improves, moves to a higher level, and succeeds. Fear commingled with cynicism regarding previous failed initiatives may have diminished their appetite for new successes to the point where it isn't visible at all, but it is still there. The desire to be a part of a success is a most powerful human motivation for a group, if it can be nurtured to the point where it reaches critical mass.

Everyone wants to be a part of a successful organization and virtually no one would intentionally choose to be a part of a failing organization. People also like shaping and determining their own future.

These two powerful human tendencies are the common ground from which we begin uniting our staff. The problem is that the staff of a school or any organization has invested themselves in trying to improve things before. Their experiences and their personalities have separated them into three typical groups, which we call "*gung-hos,*" "*go-with-the-flows,*" and "*you-can't-do-its.*"

NATURAL DIVISIONS IN A TYPICAL ORGANIZATION

In an organization that is not united by working values or a shared vision, our experience is that there are approximately 25 percent *gung-hos*, 50 percent *go-with-the-flows*, and 25 percent *you-can't-do-its*. While the undaunted *gung-hos* will jump to begin something new that has any possibility of success, the other 75 percent will vary in attitude from wary to outright negative. The *you-can't-do-it leaders* will immediately say, "We have tried this before and it doesn't work."

This is a cue for everyone to dig in their heels. Even though the *you-can't-do-its* down deep inside hope for something better and want to be a part of a success, they just don't believe it will happen—so why waste everyone's time. They will go to a blocking mentality and look for an opportunity to build their constituency and scuttle the plan.

The *go-with-the-flows* will opt first for the status quo because it is within their comfort zone—they've adjusted to present experience—even though they too hope for something better. That's why the process begins with as much as 75 percent against. The needed shift in attitude calls for doubling the number of *gung-hos* and moving many *you-can't-do-its* into the other two categories. This may seem a daunting task, but it is achievable. It happens over time.

When Ken started the process at the Doyon School, he described his staff to Nels and Joe "as the usual one-third, one-third, and one-third of positive, neutral, and negative." Two years later when Joe and Nels asked him, "How many are left in the *you-can't-do-it* group?" His answer was, "One person." How had such an overwhelming transition taken place in just two years? For two years Ken had consistently applied these four principles:

1. Organize in a way that eliminates fear;
2. Communicate in a way that builds trust and respect;
3. Encourage staff to get in touch with their positive ideals; and
4. Accomplish real achievements to shrink the doubter group.

Figure 2.1 illustrates the typical starting point of natural divisions in an organization; it then shows the initial critical mass needed to begin the process, and finally it depicts what a mature workforce looks like after working together and accomplishing meaningful achievements.

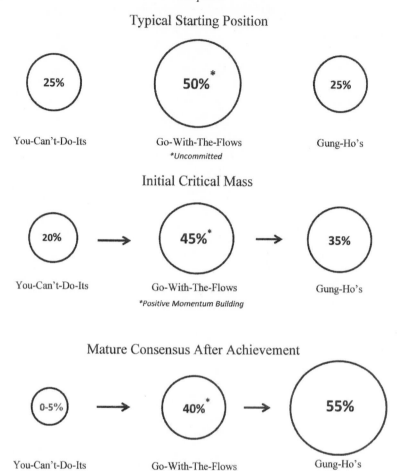

Figure 2.1. Building Consensus

"Best Workplace": A Foundational Group Exercise

Nels and Joe: "One of the important ways the leader shapes the forward movement of the process is by the questions he or she poses for group dialogue. The questions are very important. We often begin the process with a dialogue we call 'Best Workplace' (see appendix C). This dialogue is about the best place where each of us has ever worked. The establishing question and explanation go like this: *'Take a few minutes to think and then jot down a phrase or two that are the defining characteristics of the best place where you ever worked. What made it a great place to work? Workplace is very broadly defined for this exercise to include any voluntary organizations, civic groups, or teams that you have personally been a part of.'*

"We ask everyone to participate. As we go around the group listing the answers, people begin to get in touch with examples of excellence that they have experienced. It engages them. It is not abstract—it is about them and about meaningful moments in their lives.

"They share these moments with one another, revealing what is valuable to them about a workplace. They will say things like: 'I felt respected,' 'I felt a real part of things,' 'people listened to me,' 'there was good communication and no surprises,' 'we were all on the same page,' 'they were interested in what I thought and how I felt,' 'people really knew their jobs and worked well together,' 'leadership was knowledgeable and trustworthy,' etc.

"Depending on the number of people, we ask each person to contribute one or two characteristics. We ask them to talk briefly about the organization and what made it special for them. This produces a list of phrases on a board, flip chart, computer, or projector. From that list we ask the group to do a quick prioritization (see appendix D). It is valuable to know which of the characteristics posed by the various individuals are of most importance to the group as a whole. Eight to twelve defining "characteristics of a great workplace" are thus prioritized.

"The next task is to engage in a discussion regarding what we can learn from the list. *What conclusions can be drawn from the list? What does this list tell you about excellent organizations? What do we have to do to become a best workplace?* Given the opportunity to fully process the results of this exercise, participants typically come to conclusions like this: *'If we want this school to become a best workplace, we should look at how to work well together and become united behind goals we believe in.'*

"*Sharing examples of excellence from our own experience starts us down the road toward a common vision for our school's future.*

"What is amazing about this exercise is that your staff as a group already had within them a wonderfully detailed description of the characteristics of an outstanding organization—as good as you'd find in a book. Who knew? This is the first of many untapped assets that will emerge from using the combined knowledge base and wisdom of the group."

COMMITTING WORKING VALUES TO WRITING

We thought long and hard about how to improve working relationships, coming to the conclusion that we needed to put a set of working values *in writing* as the staff's promise to one another—their professional agreement—*this is who I will be for you and who I will expect you to be for me.* Working values became for us the cornerstone of building a school's working culture.

Before discussing the actual values themselves, here are some reasons that it is beneficial to commit them to writing:

- Verbal agreements are more susceptible to differences in recollection and interpretation, often meaning different things to different people, and thus opening us to disagreement and conflict.
- Written agreements clarify meanings and develop shared understanding.
- Negotiating written agreements puts differences on the table now rather than in a time of crisis.
- Each of us is freed from being interpreter and police officer of verbal meanings.
- Perceived transgressions can be referenced to the written agreements, rather than being raised personally between individuals.
- Consensus behind the written values becomes a force for cohesion.
- Written agreements are more likely to gain firm commitment and follow-through.
- Posting the values in workspaces becomes an open sign of our commitment to high-quality professional relationships.

We do not favor broad, nonspecific agreements such as "to work together in a respectful and collegial atmosphere." This type of very general agreement, while meritorious, fails to precisely identify those behaviors that would contribute to "a respectful and collegial atmosphere." The intent of the working values as we have designed them is to promote *specific positive behaviors* that build the organization and to avoid *specific negative behaviors* that are destructive of good teamwork.

Discussing and agreeing upon a set of working values has the power to immediately elevate the organization's culture.

We suggest beginning by handing out a copy of the set of values that we developed with a teacher/administrator team from the Ipswich schools (see appendix D for a one-page version). Consideration of the values begins in this way: "*The list of working values on your handout is just a discussion starter. We are free to eliminate, add to, amend, or change anything on the list. In the end it needs to be our consensus list of working values. There can be as many or few as we want. If we are to abide by these values, we need to own them.*" The process begins by looking at the starter list of values one at a time for amendment, deletion, or acceptance, afterward going on to add any additional values your staff deems important.

Even though we tell teachers and staff to freely edit the list as they see fit, most groups like the list and only do a modest amount of amending, deleting, or adding. Sometimes an additional item or two is added to address issues of special concern to a particular school.

Keep only those values that everyone accepts. When the values are accepted by unanimous consent, people try to live up to them. Everyone trying to live up to the values gives a positive upward jolt to the culture of the organization. Thereafter, it is the job of the principal and staff leaders to keep the spirit of the agreement alive.

Ken: "I recognized the need for the working values to be a living document. I sensed that the staff deeply appreciated the roadmap the values provided and the significant role they played in articulating the best of who we were and hoped to be. If there are actions that appear to fall outside the parameters of the values, remind people that they have agreed to a standard, and it works only if they live by it. Speaking with anyone who begins to violate the agreement is very important. This is best done in private, but if cause arises in a meeting you have no choice but to say politely, 'That kind of comment goes against our working values.'

"Letting violations pass without comment will gradually erode adherence to the agreement. However, if someone raises a legitimate question about the workability of a particular value, bring that issue back to the group for discussion. Reminders of the values should occasionally be a part of the leader's comments at meetings. In addition, an annual reading and review for update also helps to keep the values alive. This is important for keeping the process healthy and going."

Our set of fourteen working values follows.

WORKING VALUES FOR STAFF, TEAMS, AND MEETINGS

A team's working environment is formed by the manner in which each member participates in the process. The goal of these working values is to help members create a working environment that is productive, rewarding, and enjoyable.

Not My Ideas, But the Best Ideas: The team process is a search for improvements that work best. Come to the table in pursuit of the best ideas. If others can improve upon our ideas, we should encourage them to do so.

Be Encouraging to Others: Receiving and giving encouragement helps us to do our best. If we recognize the efforts of others and encourage each other, we will feel good about working together and are more likely to produce an excellent result.

Give Others the Respect We Want to Receive: When we speak, we want others to listen to us, having an open mind to the ideas we are presenting. We should offer others the same openness that we want. In such an atmosphere, ideas flow freely, making the process more productive.

Focus on Listening, Not Just Hearing: To listen actively is to make an effort to understand and respect another person's thoughts and feelings. If we are merely hearing, we may be thinking about our next response and miss an opportunity for understanding.

Try First to Understand, Then to Be Understood: What we already know may only be part of the information we need to make wise decisions. When we listen to others first, more facts and points of view become available, enabling us to make better choices and develop team consensus.

Maintain a Positive Attitude: Keeping a positive attitude in the face of negativity creates an environment that is positive, productive, and successful. Reacting negatively to a problem or situation only escalates it.

Be Honest and Open: Members must be able to take action on the basis of information provided by other team members. Hidden agendas break trust and destroy the team's ability to interact successfully.

Be Tough on the Issues, Easy on the People: Say what you mean, but don't say it mean. Standing up for good ideas adds real value to the process. Making our remarks personal sabotages the team's task and pushes the team toward gridlock. Focus on the issue while avoiding the personal.

Trust Goes Beyond the Meeting: Be loyal to those not present at all times. Establish working relationships built on trust and integrity. Respect for others builds a sense of confidence and community.

Preset Solutions Hinder Progress: A key to successful planning is for members to state their interests and concerns while being open and flexible as to how those interests will be achieved—leaving the process open to creative solutions.

Avoid Interpreting Others' Motivations: People will usually allow us our own thoughts and feelings without becoming defensive. It is effective to talk about what we think and feel and avoid interpreting the actions and motivations of others. People resent it and become defensive when we act as if we understand their thoughts better than they do.

Respect Diversity: Diversity contributes to the strength of our collective efforts. We each have a unique contribution to make and everyone's contribution is to be honored. We will respect the diverse paths to excellence.

Blame No One; Fix the Problem: Blame adds a second problem to the original problem. Staying respectful and on the side of others, even when they make a mistake, is critically important to good, long-term, working relationships.

Make the Team's Task Our Highest Priority: Successful teams are those that truly come together behind a mutually shared vision and goals. For this to occur, the task of the team must be given precedence over the many different personal priorities that also motivate us.

WORKING VALUES REDUCE FEAR

In looking at relationships in an organization, the goal is to build trust and confidence and reduce fear and conflict. Below is a list of fears that the working values reduce.

- People do not encourage me.
- People do not respect me.
- When things go wrong people get negative.
- There are too many hidden agendas.
- People manipulate outcomes behind your back.
- I'll look out for myself first, like everyone else does.
- People talk about you behind your back.
- You have to be at meetings to protect yourself.
- Nobody listens to me.
- Nobody is interested in my ideas; they are quick to criticize.
- Everybody is too busy selling their own ideas.
- They're all so defensive.
- People make issues personal.
- They don't ask questions, they believe they know what I'm thinking.
- They do not respect what I contribute to this organization.
- They do not appreciate my vision of excellence because it is different from theirs.
- Whenever something goes wrong they look for someone to blame.

If you have worked in an organization where even some of these fears are a real part of the "daily workings," you know how difficult that can be. It doesn't make for an enjoyable place to spend more than forty hours a week. On the other hand, we would all like to be part of an organizational culture steeped in encouragement, respect, openness, and honesty. When listening to groups engaged in the best workplace exercise, the respect they have for such high quality workplaces shines through.

We all value a workplace that welcomes our ideas, where disagreements stay objective, where we focus on the issues, avoid blaming, look for creative solutions together, and respect diversity. If this sounds too good to be true, we suggest that there are many well-run organizations with excellent cultures where leadership encourages participation and respectful treatment, and where the employees "buy in" to this way of interacting. You will hear all about such organizations when you do the best workplace exercise with your staff.

Diana Minton, who prior to her retirement was the director of special education programs in the Ipswich schools, offers a powerful example of the contrast in working cultures that can be found in different organizations.

Diana: "At administrative meetings in the Ipswich schools, you can joke, laugh, feel frustrated, and be angry. You are received with empathy and support. People pitch in to make things right. We are always trying to make things better for our students. That is our focus. This atmosphere allows us to fashion and execute new plans for improvement without feeling threatened.

"I contrast this with a school district I worked in years ago. There I had to prepare myself mentally and physically to handle the stress of merely attending a meeting of the administrative team. It was tense and a trial. Several of the people at these meetings would viciously turn on you and attack, with little if any provocation. People would scheme between meetings. Meetings were often stage-managed performances set up in advance. Information given at meetings was completely unreliable. We were constantly called on to take sides in the ensuing battles. The environment was deeply toxic.

"*All we could do in that district was to do what we did yesterday—and lucky to do that.* How could you create something new and better? Who could you rely on for support to help make a new initiative a success? The one thing you could be sure of was that there were fellow administrators ready to rip you apart if you tried something new and failed—or even faltered."

The culture of any organization is created by the choices of the leadership and the people who work there. Working values help us to make better choices both individually and collectively.

THE OPPOSITE OF FEAR IS TRUST

People can be afraid of each other or they can trust each other. In a normal situation at work we are probably doing some of both—choosing some people to trust while being wary of others. The most traumatic fear that people can experience is for their physical safety. Fear in the workplace is not typically about physical safety, but is more likely a fear of being placed in situations of emotional discomfort or situations where our status, self-esteem, or position is at risk.

This fear of discomfort or loss can be felt just as intensely as a threat to personal safety, due to the inaccuracy of emotional associations in our brain. The emotional system in the brain can, and often does, escalate fear of discomfort or loss to a place where it feels like our survival is at stake.

The antidote for fear in the workplace is trust. Whenever we build trust in a group of people, we are at the same time diminishing the amount of fear that is present.

These are some of the building blocks on which trust is built: sincerity, honesty, integrity, fairness, openness, empathy, support, and encouragement. Acting in any of these ways builds trust.

Consider this question, "Can you have excellent, effective working relationships without trust?" For many reasons, the answer is "no." Trust allows us to act based on the other person's words. If they speak and there is trust, we feel free to act. What kind of relationship do we have if we are hesitant to act based on the word of a coworker (i.e., if we find ourselves checking for hidden meanings, pondering over possible insincerities or manipulations, and worrying about potentially misleading facts before responding)? What does it signify if we won't act without covering our back? Does this make for timely, enthusiastic teamwork, or does it make for guarded action or no action at all? *One thing is for sure, it doesn't make for great results.* The remedy for organizations rife with fear is to build trust.

Joe: "There are few more important sections in this book than this one on trust. Employees yearn for a leader they can trust. We can't list all the ways a leader might violate trust, but we want to put the spotlight on two that stick out.

1. *Having two conversations in our mind.* In this case, a leader tells people what he or she wants, or commissions an initiative, but has a second unrevealed conversation going on in his or her head pertaining to the real reason for initiating the action. The first conversation is with our coworkers, and the second conversation is the one we are keeping to ourselves pertaining to the real reason we are asking people to act. An example comes to mind that affected me personally (I guess it has been burned into my psyche), where I was part of a committee that did excellent work, that reconciled diverse and contentious groups, and that felt that we had 'really done our job.'

   After reporting, however, the group felt betrayed when there was no follow-through by the leaders who had formed the committee. The reason, as it turned out, was that forming the committee was only an effort to placate certain vocal groups, to grease the squeaky wheel, and to 'buy time.' In the end there had never been a real intention of following up and advocating for resources to implement the committee report. Here's the big point that leaders who engage in hidden internal conversations forget: *People always find out.* Then they stop acting on your word.

2. *Being obsessed about getting what we want.* In this second instance, leaders are honestly expressing the conversation that is in their mind. The problem occurs when leaders regard what they want for the school as something that *must happen*, to the degree that it causes them to lose perspective. They stop listening. They insist on getting what they want and become unaware of the feelings they might be hurting, or of the disrespect they might be showing. Even if what the leaders want to do is 'right,' people will feel trod upon, while the

leaders, in their effort to attain the all-important outcome, become oblivious to the long-term negative impact of their actions.

The antidote for actions that cause mistrust is to do everything we can as leaders to remain thoughtful, objective, and trustworthy about our internal conversations."

W. Timothy Gallwey wrote a brilliant book that provided a revealing look inside the minds of tennis players (and many other people) called *The Inner Game of Tennis*. Gallwey gives leaders good advice when he says, "The ghosts of the past and the monsters of the future disappear when all of one's conscious energy is employed in understanding the present."

HOW DO WE SEE OUR STAFF?

It becomes easier to trust when we fully appreciate the people who work with us. How we see our staff determines the tenor of the leadership we will provide. If we look at our people in a narrow way, we see worker skills and employees. That is fine as far as it goes. But what we really have in our staff is every book they have ever read, every teacher who ever taught them, every piece of knowledge conveyed to them, every person who ever gave them good advice, everything they've learned from prior work experiences, and all the experiences from all the people they've met and places they've been.

We call this the "*knowledge base*" of the people in our employ. It is a wide and deep resource and each staff member brings the total sum of his or her own unique package to the workplace every day. The depth of what we have in our people is not visible on the outside.

The people we work with have within them enormous reservoirs of leadership, information, ability, energy, and creativity—reservoirs that may, in large part, be going untapped.

Some leaders completely supplant this incredible resource by relying mostly on their own knowledge and ideas. It makes more sense to us to utilize the creativity and wisdom available in the school's workforce.

There is a teamwork exercise that goes like this: "*In the next minute I want you to write down any possible use you can think of for this ordinary paper drinking cup*" (see appendix C). At the end of the minute, and after results are compiled, we typically find that almost no one comes up with more than fourteen uses. The group as a whole, meanwhile, depending on size, will often compile thirty or forty different uses for the cup. As a school considers its future and discusses how to improve, doesn't it make sense to have three times as many options for finding creative solutions and for making wise decisions? That is just one aspect of what collaboration offers.

As if using the group's collective knowledge base wasn't enough, there is the dynamic of "piggybacking" off each other's ideas and energies, thus leveraging the ingenuity and power of our individual efforts. In a collaborative environment, creativity and enthusiasm are transmitted and "caught," from person to person.

The ability of a leader to cultivate effective teamwork begins with how the leader sees the people he or she works with. Who are they in our mind's eye? What is our default mindset when we see them? Gandhi moved the people of a continent from a subservient mentality to stand up and declare themselves free. According to Louis Fischer, his biographer, Gandhi viewed people as if all that was in them was the best that was in them. He brought out the best in people because he was looking for it.

Our experience is that leaders' inner view of their staff tends to become a self-fulfilling prophecy: Those who look for the "something more" in people are those who find it. Believing in people and valuing their input is a part of helping them get in touch with the powerful positive tendencies they hold within.

Nels: "When we began trying to convert our supervisors at Sylvania to use teamwork, I'll admit to believing that some of the 'old school' supervisors would never get it. I was very surprised when it turned out that not only did some of these old-fashioned supervisors 'get it,' but they became leaders and advocates of teamwork. They became great allies to have in your camp. This leads me to say, when you begin a teamwork process, *do not write anyone off in your mind.* How you see them in your mind will influence what you say and do when interacting with them. Their response and participation will become a reflection of what you are thinking about them."

Write no one off. Have the attitude that what we are doing in this process makes so much sense that eventually everyone will want to join in.

Treat every person in a way that shows your belief in their ability to become a contributor to a successful improvement process—even if at the start they are the staunchest members of the *"you-can't-do-it"* group. The satisfaction that emerges from successful collaboration is so meaningful to people that you are likely to be surprised by who becomes your ally in the end.

"WHAT GOES" IN OUR ENVIRONMENT?

Joe: "We are well aware that people can be very negative. People also can be very positive—the same people. In every environment, leadership and membership explicitly or tacitly establish 'what goes' and 'what does not go' in that environment. The staff will play the game according to the 'rules' that exist.

As a freshly minted, highly enthusiastic young second lieutenant in the Marine Corps, I took my first assignment as an infantry platoon leader in the First Marine Brigade in Hawaii. It was a shock to me to see a company next door that looked sloppy in dress, in drill, and in almost all they did. Other companies that I saw, including my own, lived up to my expectations. I look back with embarrassment (I was twenty-three years old) that my first belief about that company next door was that they had somehow managed to collect most of the 'misfits and screw-ups' in the Marine Corps.

A couple of months later, they got a new company commander. Within weeks, those same 'misfits and screw-ups' were polishing their boots, looking good in drill, and hustling around in their training regimens doing an excellent job; sloppiness and lack of effort 'didn't go' any longer in the leadership environment created by the new company commander. It was the same group of men!

Sometimes when I hear politicians talking about changing all the teachers in a school, I am reminded of that example. A few teachers should transition to another profession, but most teachers are sufficiently skilled and sincerely care about the children they teach to be a part of a successful school. They are capable of functioning at a high level, if the educational system in their school fosters such a result. This belief is reflected in TQM guru W. Edwards Deming's frequent declaration that 85 percent of organizational failures are system failures not attributable to people. While Deming credited Joseph Juran for this statement, he later upped the number to 95 percent at his seminars, according to Myron Tribus, who worked with Deming.

Even when it seems as if it is the person who failed, a second look will often reveal that he or she was the victim of poor training or had the misfortune of operating in a poorly designed or managed system."

Our first priority should be to propel the teachers we have toward excellence by inspiring them and helping them to become part of an outstanding team and system; only then should we look at individuals who may remain in the underperforming category. It makes more sense to use our best efforts to elevate the entire group first (because you might be surprised by who moves up!).

BUILDING UPON POWERFUL POSITIVE HUMAN TENDENCIES

If we are to build a powerful working environment, our task is to enhance positive tendencies while minimizing the negative ones. Feed the plants and minimize the weeds. Harnessing positive human tendencies is a powerful way to build a culture of achievement. The following list reviews some of the positive human tendencies we have discussed in this chapter.

People want to

- be a part of a success;
- control their own destiny;
- unite behind a group process that is forward looking;
- have an opportunity to be creative;
- build something they can be proud of;
- work in an environment free of fear and blame;
- be respected and valued;
- be able to trust and rely on the people around them;
- have transparent dealings with others;
- be treated with patience, understanding, empathy, compassion, and encouragement;
- contribute to a powerful group knowledge base;
- be acknowledged for their abilities and participation;
- get in touch with their own personal visions of excellence;
- find that unique special something more that is in them and others; and
- achieve good things for students.

Now you might be thinking, "It will be hard to get such tendencies to become a reality given how my school or organization functions." That is not the case. Please get rid of those doubts. The Doyon School and many other organizations that have successfully implemented the type of teamwork process we describe were far from unique places at the start.

A REVIEW OF CHAPTER 2 CONCEPTS

- People are not afraid of change; they are afraid of being hurt.
- People want to be a part of a success and to shape their own future.
- People have a depth of rich experiences; this knowledge base can be a powerful resource and ally in building a great organization.
- Don't get mired in blame; turn dialogue forward to solutions that unite the group.
- Constantly work to diminish fear and build trust.
- Positive working relationships free our staff to focus on accomplishing goals.
- Leaders' views of their staff tends to become a self-fulfilling prophecy. Write no one off. Have the attitude that what we are doing makes so much sense that eventually everyone will want to join in.
- Pay careful attention to building an initial positive critical mass from within the gung-hos, go-with-the-flows, and even a few you-can't-do-its.

- Dialogue questions that call for sharing positive personal experiences begin the process of building a mutual vision.
- Agreeing to a set of working values immediately elevates the school's culture.
- Working values promote specific positive behaviors that build the organization and help us avoid specific negative behaviors that are destructive to good teamwork.
- Leadership overtly or tacitly sets the tone for "what goes" in any organization.
- Elevate the entire environment first; then see who is left in the underperforming category.

Chapter Three

Becoming a Collaborative Leader

WHAT IS YOUR TOP PRIORITY AS A LEADER?

Let's start with a crucial question: "Can a leader unite a school behind an overriding goal that he or she does not strongly hold?" Our answer is a clear "NO."

As leaders, we won't be able to unite our staff around "producing good results in the lives of students," unless that is actually, at the deepest level, our own top priority.

Your opportunity to accomplish something special as a leader begins with giving yourself over to what some might see as a sappy ideal. Forget school politics, forget focusing on personal advancement, forget past failures, forget being reserved, cool, or cynical; instead, give yourself over to the ideal of producing good results in the lives of your students. *If the ideal doesn't come alive in you it won't come alive in those you are leading.*

You can't fake it; there can't be another agenda; people are too smart for that and will see through it. If you have reached or are aspiring to a leadership position, this is your time to make a real difference. Focusing on the vision of helping students is the first and best way you can provide direction for your school. Because you are the leader, and it's what you are all about, it rubs off. Be aware that this cannot be a "wishful priority" because if it is, when push comes to shove, it will be abandoned or replaced with something else.

For it to drive the school, it must first drive you. It doesn't matter that it didn't drive you before; it only counts that it genuinely drives you now.

FUNCTIONING AT THE VISION LEVEL

For a leader to guide the organization toward greatness, he or she must lead that organization to the "vision level." The key to achieving the vision level is for everyone to be on the same page, working enthusiastically together for the same positive purpose.

The three levels we describe below are really a continuum rather than discrete and separate. They represent a spectrum that runs from *organizational heaven* (the top of the vision level) to *organizational hell* (the bottom of the dysfunctional level).

- *Vision Level:* Virtually everyone is working together for the same purpose. The goals are well chosen and make a palpable difference. The staff is enthusiastic and energized. Excellence and optimism are pervasive. There is genuine collegiality, mutual support, and a transparent search to find and implement the best ideas.
- *Normal Level:* Good results are achieved occasionally but without an overriding sense of unity or common purpose. Social interaction is spiced with gossip and cliques. The focus is often on "doing what we did yesterday." Leadership may be pushing the latest silver bullet, but support is undermined by cynicism since none of the previous "bullets" has made a substantial difference. The staff is divided into "gung-hos," "go-with-the-flows," and "you-can't-do-its." New initiatives are met with some enthusiasm, some compliance, and some sabotage.
- *Dysfunctional Level:* Personal ambition and biases reign supreme. Motivation is related to self-interest. The leader tries to stay in control and look good. Others seek to protect their job or make a name for themselves. Favoritism is rampant. There is a great deal of drama. People push their own agendas and are willing to stab others in the back to get ahead. If things go wrong, the search is on for someone to blame. The organization's long-term success is at best a secondary consideration. Many of the working values are present but turned upside down in the negative.

Where an organization falls along the above spectrum is determined by the quality of its leadership. Our task is to help you to position your organization to function at the vision level. Everything in this book is aimed at helping you get there.

PROVIDING ORGANIZATIONAL DIRECTION

Joe: "I served as a Marine infantry platoon commander in the first year of the Vietnam War. From there I was sent to be a recruit training officer at Parris

Island, South Carolina. I became a series commander, which meant that I supervised a training unit called a 'Series' consisting of thirteen drill instructors and 344 recruits from the start of training through graduation.

"The 'pick-up meeting' was a briefing presented to the series drill instructors and commander prior to the start of training. I went to my first pick-up meeting, held in a classroom on a typically hot day at Parris Island, not knowing what to expect. I sat at the back. The battalion commander, company commander, and the company gunnery sergeant each proceeded to give their briefing, answered questions, and left. Their comments were mostly made up of administrative concerns and a list of 'do nots.'

"The thirteen drill instructors in front of me stood up to leave. I said, 'Excuse me, gentlemen, but I'd like to make a few brief remarks as well.' They sat down and I went on to say, 'I know I'm new here. I also know that everything you just heard is important in making this base run well. I expect you to pay attention to these things and do them well. However, our first job is to train outstanding Marines and that is what I will be paying the most attention to. Many of these men will be going into combat and it is our job to make sure they are ready.' *I was consciously calling for a shift in focus, away from administration and toward excellence in training.*

"I subsequently found that several of the most capable senior drill instructors were a bit burned out—it is a grinding job and they had been at it for a while. The shift in focus toward operational excellence suited them fine; it ignited some positive refocusing and a resulting return to top performance by these highly competent drill instructors.

"*What you talk about reveals your highest priorities.* An emphasis on training excellence remained my consistent focus. We constantly sought ways to improve our training regimes. The fifth and final unit I led (my tour was ending) was the only recruit unit in three years to win all of the awards that could be presented to a Series at Parris Island. That accomplishment did not happen because I was a great leader. I am not. It happened because I refocused everyone in my unit on what mattered most. The ideal of producing great Marines is a vision we could share. It inspired them, helped them to rise above the grind, and pulled them together. It freed them to do their best. They did the rest."

Organizations might be focused on any or all of the following: getting through the day; doing what we did yesterday; putting out fires; reconciling conflicting personal agendas; dealing with factions competing for influence; pleasing the boss; griping about working conditions; protecting our job or reputation; competing for funding (or complaining about the lack of it); gossiping and in-fighting; and acting to get ahead personally.

Having such diverse and competing focuses is like hitching teams of horses to all four sides of a wagon and asking all the horses to pull at once. When the wagon goes nowhere you might think the horses have to be whipped harder to get things moving. All that would accomplish is to tear the wagon apart. Progress calls for focus. Decide where you want to go together, hitch all the horses up to the front of the wagon, and pull it in that direction. Sounds easy, but it isn't.

How do we focus a school that may be simultaneously juggling a number of the above organizational preoccupations? *The first thing is to recognize that we need a uniting vision—one that is outside of and above personal interest.* We could not reconcile the egos of a staff of 100 persons if we had a thousand years. But we can unite people outside of their egos by getting them to put aside egos for a purpose greater than self.

A *vision*, if it is appealing, unites. Teachers did not get into teaching to get rich. For the most part, they came to make a difference in the lives of young people. It is natural for this ideal to be at the core of an overriding vision capable of uniting them. *We believe the only focus capable of pulling everyone together in a school is the desire to produce outstanding results in the lives of students.*

Keep the spotlight on doing what is best for students. Keep coming back to that student-centered focus whenever you meet. The same is done in business when successful companies focus their workforce on producing a great product or service. Don't let all the stuff that comes your way cloud your vision or get it turned around. The leader is the one who has to center or re-center everyone when such events and difficulties threaten to turn their attention elsewhere. If we as leaders are ambivalent regarding the reason for our efforts, we open the door to a host of competing and distracting priorities—and as Yogi Berra said, "If you don't know where you're going, you might wind up someplace else."

LEADERSHIP IN STYLE AND PRINCIPLE

Is there a formula for leadership that will ensure that your school gets to the vision level? The answer is both "no" and "yes." No, collaborative leadership doesn't call for or require a particular personal *style*; but yes, there are fundamental leadership *principles* essential to success.

Barry Cahill and Cheryl Forster were both successful, veteran school principals before they married. If you ask people familiar with their work, they are likely to tell you that Barry and Cheryl are markedly different in their approach to leadership. Cheryl, Ipswich's middle school principal (recently retired), is a high-energy person and a strong believer in personal connections. Any student in trouble got her personal attention and empathy. If the student's home life was a disaster and, for instance, they needed a pair of shoes—she'd go out and buy them.

Cheryl is all about relationships. Barry, Ipswich's high school principal (also recently retired), led with a less personal, more formal style, creating and standing behind consistent rules and practices that guided the operation of the school. Despite their differences, each won awards for leadership.

Their differences are what showed on the outside. A closer look reveals that they had more in common than meets the eye. We discovered this by interviewing them separately and unrehearsed on the subject of "keys to good school leadership."

Here is a condensed version of Cheryl's keys to successful school leadership.

- A school gets very mixed up whenever it fails to put kids first; something may be right for the adults but not be what is best for kids.
- Sticks to what's right despite setbacks; good things don't always come easily.
- Exemplify energy, vision, and a can-do attitude; model "we can do this."
- People have to know where they stand; inconsistency creates doubt; being fair is a big part of building trust.
- Empathy is also a big part of trust; ask whether you want to be treated this way.
- Kindness and empathy are contagious; it's up to the leader to model them.
- People have to trust the information you are giving, and know that it's safe to go where you are leading.
- Never leave an information void; it gets filled with false information.
- We don't do "flap", drama makes problems worse.
- I will challenge anyone who wants to make our culture toxic or sabotage group decisions; people shouldn't have to work in a toxic or dysfunctional culture.

Here is a condensed version of Barry's keys to successful school leadership.

- Be strongly committed to doing the right thing for kids.
- Recognize that the most important part of a principal's job is leadership, not management—be a leader.
- Be tenacious; don't be afraid to try because something is hard to do.
- The job is to drive change, not do it yourself, and if the ball gets off track get it back on, but don't be pushing the ball by yourself.
- Your people have to have confidence in your calmness and ethical foundation; be a person others can respect and rely on when things are difficult.
- Don't overreact; be calm and thoughtful in your words and actions.
- I want people in my building to see that I am well intentioned and genuinely interested in them.

- Be honest in all your dealings; treat teachers and students consistently; you can't play favorites; be consistent day to day.
- Provide a sense of safety for teachers, staff, and students; all need to feel safe at our school.
- Develop personal but not private relationships; your people should be able to share their concerns with you; if they share something it cannot come back to them from others.
- Be true to who you are.

An Ipswich teacher who heard that we had interviewed Cheryl and Barry on the subject of leadership asked, "Did you find anything in common?" (expecting the answer to be no). The answer, unexpectedly, was a strong "yes." Two people who might appear, even to their own faculties, to have such different leadership styles, had in fact, a *common inner vision* of school leadership.

Both put kids first and encouraged others to do the same; both hold a strong vision of themselves as a leader who would be respected and who respects others; both work at being a leader who acts consistently with equanimity and fairness—someone who can be trusted; both are not afraid to lead; both want everyone in their building to feel safe; both expect difficulties to occur and respond to them with determination; both have a "can do" attitude; and both are consistently and consciously channeling energy toward building a strong culture and a school-wide commitment to progress. In actuality, despite stylistic differences, they share the most meaningful and important components of the job.

In these two highly successful principals we have an excellent example of different leadership styles, both of which work. Some of us are outgoing and bubbly, while others are more reserved and introspective; some of us are dynamic, while others are more deliberate and methodical. As Barry said, be true to who you are. Each approach can be an asset.

At the same time, it is essential to have at our core a set of deeply held principles that guide our leadership. Think through and write down the guiding principles you want to exemplify. Outstanding leaders are guided by strong inner visions. Over time their staff will discover and align with that inner vision if led consistently and if the vision is a worthy one. Successful collaborative leadership is not a God-given gift, nor is it a matter of personality; it can be *intentionally* developed by someone wishing to grow into an effective leader.

RELATING TO OTHERS

Building confidence in our leadership, and engaging people in our vision, begins with how we encounter and relate to others. Our "persona"—the image we project—should not be a cloak we put on, or a facade we conjure up for others. It should be "real," the same on the inside as what is seen on the outside. Cheryl and Barry both come across as real and authentic people.

The following are five personal leadership characteristics that cultivate positive professional connections.

- *Personable*: Smiling sets an immediate tone that you see others as important.
- *Attentive:* Be a good listener and take time to hear what others have to say.
- *Encouraging:* Look for, notice, and name all the good things your staff is doing. Establish a 4:1 or 5:1 environment of positive to corrective comments.
- *Trustworthy:* Do what is right in the right way. Do not curry favor with others. Be fair and consistent to all, with no hidden agendas. Be open and honest. Allow others to feel comfortable that you will not turn on them, even when times are tough. Your word must be reliable in order for others to take action based solely on what you say.
- *Confident:* Let your staff know that there is nothing that can't be faced together, that together we will respond to all challenges in an intelligent, thoughtful way, doing our best. In the end, that's all anyone can do and it is enough.

THE IMPORTANCE OF SCHEDULING TIME FOR IMPROVEMENT PLANNING

Although it is rarely acknowledged, the typical method of operation we have seen in schools is essentially maintaining the status quo by repeating the past while providing small amounts of time to plan for the future. Like many organizational dynamics, this isn't being done maliciously or even consciously. We work hard producing each day's education and do what we can to make things better in the little time that is left over. That's just the reality of things—or so it seems.

Improvement often gets the time that is left over after regular operations. This reality is at the root of why many improvement efforts are seen by employees as sporadic and not a high priority for leadership. Improvement planning needs to be scheduled as a valued part of regular operations. Doing this gives improvement efforts an all-new legitimacy and dynamism.

One school Nels and Joe worked with had a contract restricting the time that the principal could meet with the faculty to a maximum of twenty-four hours in the entire school year. In order to be successful in making improvements, the principal specifically designated twelve of those twenty-four hours for the improvement process, and solicited volunteers to do research and organizing between meetings. As it turned out, even that modest amount of time systematically woven into regular operations produced excellent results!

If you want your school to improve, add improvement to the schedule. If improvement isn't allotted a regular place in the operating schedule, year in and year out, the results will never satisfy because the change will not be of a sufficient magnitude to produce a sense of accomplishment. A serious effort at school improvement calls for time to be set aside, with required attendance by all at key decision points.

Some districts may need to adjust their labor contracts to allow sufficient time to obtain staff participation in improvement planning. The alternative is to do the planning without the participation of those who are closest to the students. Maximize the usefulness of whatever time you have by finding ways to dispense with administrivia. Do whatever you can to clear time each month to plan for improvement.

WORK ON WHAT IS IMPORTANT

Improvement time is hard to come by. Leaders should be vigilant lest the school's improvement energies be directed at solving problems that are too small in scope to affect the school at its core. We don't want our improvement effort to be one of running around oiling squeaky wheels. When we target areas for improvement we want to make the selection based on the following premise: *We have limited time, resources, and energies that can be allocated toward improvement initiatives, so let's select initiatives that will produce the greatest benefit for students and the greatest results for our efforts.*

Once we recognize that the time we have for improvement is *finite*, it becomes critically important to prioritize what we hope to accomplish. This is another of those concepts that may evoke a "tell me something new" reaction, until you look at typical school improvement plans that contain 20–25 goals and that are clearly based on the flawed premise that everything can be done simultaneously.

Ken: "If your school system is as short of funds as ours, you might agree that your primary investment in improvement is going to be 'sweat equity'— that makes choosing improvement goals all about 'bang for sweat equity.' The Doyon School chose to begin its improvement process with its reading program. Many negatives were displaced by the creation of this powerful new positive—a consistent, effective reading program, spiraling upward from grade to grade.

"Not only were other academic achievements built upon that new reading program, it also displaced negatives (e.g., fewer students being discouraged, fewer parents upset at seeing their child falling behind grade level, and fewer emotional and behavioral issues that accompany student failure). It was a goal worthy of our time."

STRENGTHS FIX WEAKNESSES

As an example of strengths fixing weaknesses, let's say that a staff is experiencing a lot of friction among its members. While it is a good thing to want to bring a quick halt to unprofessional behavior (and it should be done), if that is all we do, it's too narrow a scope and will produce too narrow a result. Stopping negatives focuses on what *not to do*, but fails to tell us what *to do* if we want a great workplace. The process of adopting a set of working values, and then doing all we can to live up to them, is the type of positive action that takes us well beyond redressing negative behaviors.

The most meaningful results are achieved not merely by contending with negatives, but by creating greater positives that naturally displace them.

For instance, if there is too much fighting, teasing, or bullying among students, it is imperative that it stop. But the greater result is achieved when students learn empathy and feel a sense of community with their fellow students, so they no longer want to fight, tease, or bully.

Any area of weakness may require triage. Stopping the bleeding, stopping the harm, is an important step, but is only the beginning of truly making things right. Let's say that some of your teachers are worried that other teachers are inflating grades. It is one thing to mention the problem, speak against grade inflation, and try to encourage the faculty to grade more consistently. It is a whole other thing to receive common training in assessing student work and to engage in a professional dialogue that results in uniform and consistent assessment practices. The latter constructs a positive strength within your educational system that elevates while counteracting the problem behavior. Everything you do to instill strong positives into your school's educational system is at the same time most productively diminishing negatives.

SEEK HIGH EMPOWERMENT AND HIGH ALIGNMENT

Ken: "The importance of the interplay between *empowerment of staff* and *alignment of efforts* had never crossed my mind until Joe and Nels brought those specific elements to my attention. After years of experiencing empowerment and alignment in action, I now understand that these two dynamics play a crucial and interactive role in influencing and even determining the degree of success of any organization's improvement efforts. Here are four positions where an organization may find itself:

- *Low Empowerment and Low Alignment*: If this is the status in an organization, it signals that no one really cares. The organization is drifting. Schools with this profile are invariably places of discouragement and low morale for both staff and students.
- *High Empowerment and Low Alignment*: Teachers generally respond favorably to being informed that they are going to be 'empowered,' and that they will have more decision-making power. But when high empowerment is coupled with little or no alignment, it not only suggests an inappropriate abdication of administrative responsibility; it can also have serious negative consequences for all aspects of the school's functioning—especially the cumulative effectiveness of the instructional program.
- *Low Empowerment and High Alignment*: In its 'pure' form, this is top-down 'boss' leadership. The leadership hierarchy is oblivious to seeking input from staff, and teachers get used to doing 'what they are told.' Many years ago, I worked as a grade six classroom teacher for a principal who had retired from a career as an officer in the U.S. Army. He had a definite 'top-down' leadership style. One year at the first staff meeting, after I had worked all summer preparing lessons to complement the social studies curriculum and textbook, the principal announced that the curriculum and the text had been changed over the summer.

    I was so upset I had to excuse myself from the meeting. I later found out he asked a colleague, 'What's the matter with Cooper?' It wasn't that he didn't care that I was upset; it just never occurred to him that this type of unilateral action would be so disempowering and discouraging for staff.
- *High Empowerment and High Alignment*: This is where we want to be. This is the target area. As we move toward a model of high empowerment and high alignment, we are maximizing staff input, investment, and enthusiasm on behalf of clear, focused, and prioritized goal areas. An organization doesn't arrive here by accident. The leadership must intentionally engage staff in a thoughtfully constructed process of consensus-driven prioritization. The principal is coach, coordinator, cheerleader, process director, gatekeeper, provider of resources, and now a *leader of leaders*. Becoming a leader of leaders is a great target to aspire to and an even greater destination to reach.

One additional note regarding *high alignment*: While one aspect of our intent is certainly to promote coordinated and consistent implementation of high

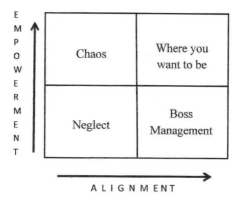

Figure 3.1. Alignment & Empowerment

quality instructional programs, I regularly reminded staff that there was to be no 'cookie cutter' curricula in our school. My expectation was that while most of the time what was taught would reflect the core curriculum and our consensus decisions, it was fine, expected, and even desirable that at other times what was taught would reflect the individual skills, strengths, talents, and interests that each teacher brought to the job. (This is similar in concept to what companies like Google do by explicitly encouraging employees to set aside time for development of their own creative ideas.)

"Each teacher has unique gifts and experiences. We wanted students to be enriched by these gifts and experiences. Passion is remembered! Emotions enhance memory; that's the way the brain works.

"Whenever we hired a new teacher, the orientation packet they received included the diagram shown in figure 3.1. We also reviewed this image each year during one of the first staff meetings. *As is the case with working values, periodic revisiting and reminders is an absolute necessity for maintaining the awareness and appreciation of our vital processes.*

"*Maximizing the staff's sense of creativity and personal ownership, while also strengthening program consistency and coordination, are not competing interests.* Both are equally necessary for organizational excellence. Striking a careful balance between 'empowerment and alignment' will allow the level of both to be high."

KNOW THE PROCESS STEPS IN ADVANCE

One of a leader's most important tasks is that of facilitating discussions around the planning process itself. We offer the following thoughts to increase the likelihood that those conversations will be productive and end well.

Creating a step-by-step process for improvement planning is like getting ready for a driving trip from Los Angeles to Boston. We pick a route, note the key milestones, make a timeline, and plan interesting stopping points. Because we plan in this way, we are less likely to have a stressful trip and more likely to arrive on time.

Again, this may sound elementary. It isn't. Teams or committees often begin without a roadmap. Without a set of process steps, the likelihood of reaching our destination is diminished. The planning process could be blown up in the middle when it hits the inevitable wall. Halfway through, frustrated parties might say, "Let's start all over again," or some members of the group may suggest going in an all-new direction in midprocess; or the group may spin its wheels for months and end up with more questions than it started with; or we might fail to keep the leaders who commissioned us up to speed and when we report back they virtually throw out our months of work and begin the discussion over from the start.

Sound familiar? These things happen—we've experienced them firsthand. Each is capable of destroying a staff's confidence in their ability to improve.

Agreeing to a written set of process steps at the start of an improvement planning initiative increases the likelihood of success.

When the group agrees to a set of steps, everyone becomes fully aware of the plan for moving forward. That knowledge greatly reduces fear. The unknown generates fear. In the unknown, all fearful thoughts can take on an air of reality. The discussion of the steps need not be lengthy. We are not looking for written perfection here, just a set of steps to get us where we want to go—or at least to the first milestone, where we can create a new set of steps to get to the second milestone.

Trust and confidence begin to build when the group comes to regard the steps as sensible and likely to get them to the finish line. The leader should add a promise when reaching agreement on the process steps: *"No step of this process will be finalized without the consensus of the group."* Because they know where and how they are going, because they know they will have a voice all along the way, your staff will make further shifts out of the "you-can't-do-it" or "go-with-the-flow" groups.

The planning and problem-solving processes presented in appendix H are tried and proven as guides to framing process steps. If followed, they are likely to lead to a successful result because they include the factors that make for good decisions.

When a team is appointed to pursue a goal or objective, sit down with them and agree on a set of process steps. Create clear answers to the questions, "Where are we going and how do we plan to get there?" When this is done, everyone can relax and put their energy into participating; it is an important part of building trust and confidence to a level that releases group energy.

THE NATURE OF THE DIALOGUE AFFECTS THE OUTCOME

When a stone is thrown into a calm pond, it causes an expanding series of ripples. Like the stone's ripples, improvement ideas in a good system should also ripple outward in an expanding dialogue.

As the improvement dialogue expands, it is important to avoid the appearance of one group selling their ideas to another.

As we discussed in the first chapter, the "selling of ideas" method of bringing initiatives forward doesn't engage your work force. The receiving group does not come to "own" the ideas. For purposes of understanding, let's look at a typical set of process steps and see how the problem of selling ideas can come into play.

In a typical planning process, we might first survey the faculty. Next, we might ask the faculty, based on the survey, to evaluate and list our school's strengths and weaknesses. Then we might ask them to prioritize the areas for improvement that resulted from the survey and the strengths/weaknesses discussion. Next, a smaller subteam might be used to bring back a "causal analysis" and take the first crack at creating options for improvement. After that, the dialogue comes back to the whole faculty and principal. The faculty and principal, in turn, will bring their thoughts to the school council, nonfaculty staff, and parent groups as they deem appropriate—if these groups have a role in implementing the plan.

At each of the transfer points in the above expanding dialogue, it is critical that the originating group not present their ideas as something they are asking the full group to rubber stamp, or to approve or reject, but only as a starting point for further discussion.

This method of expanding the dialogue keeps people out of entrenched or defensive positions. Each reporting group says, "This is what we came up with as a starting point for today's discussion." There is no threat inherent in this approach; instead, what emerges is an implicit respect for the group receiving the information. If as a result of their research, the reporting group favors one particular option; that can be shared and the reasons presented. Other viable options and data should be offered as well, so that it doesn't appear that the reporting group is backing the receiving group into a corner.

OBJECTIVITY REVEALS THE BEST SOLUTIONS

Another salient aspect of the expanding dialogue is the importance of it remaining objective and impersonal for as long as possible. If we can keep people out of hardened positions long enough, the truth of a situation will often bubble to the surface and unite them.

Nels and Joe: "We have helped to unite groups that were extremely diverse in their orientation toward a topic by emphasizing the importance of objectivity when structuring the process. A good example is a project we did with the Ipswich High School principal, Barry Cahill. The question of whether to have a school schedule made up of shorter or longer time blocks had divided the high school faculty for years before Barry was hired as principal.

"It was important to Barry that this issue be resolved in a manner that would allow the faculty to take ownership of the new schedule. Early in the process, the faculty agreed to use weighted criteria, deciding to give double weight to choosing a schedule that would be 'best for students' and single weight to 'best for the faculty' and 'best for the school district.' Immediately, that began moving people out of personal, emotion-backed positions.

"Whenever what is 'best for students' is made the top priority, it starts moving people toward objectivity and away from divisive personal positioning.

"We worked with Principal Cahill to design process steps that developed and explored scheduling options as objectively as possible. The faculty focused on researching and creating a list of possible schedule formats without taking positions. They were then asked to evaluate the scheduling options, again in an objective way, by generating a list of 'pros' and 'cons' for each option.

"Once the dialogue was structured in this way, we saw teachers putting up cons on the very ideas that they had spent years arguing for. The teachers deserve a great deal of credit for the way that they conducted themselves. The upshot of the story is that after a total of five months of objective work by the faculty (which included visiting other schools and creating hypothetical schedules), they were able to decide on a new schedule by consensus, without ever having an argument or needing a formal vote."

Roger Fisher and William Ury wrote *Getting to Yes*, and Ury wrote *Getting Past No*—two great books on the techniques of negotiation and problem resolution. Ury counsels us that when we face a critical negotiation we need to step back, collect our wits, and see the situation objectively. He recommends that we "go to the balcony," which is a metaphor for adopting a neutral attitude of detachment. The success we describe above in helping the teachers reach consensus resolution regarding their school's schedule was a process where we asked the group to remain on the "the balcony of objectivity" for the entire process.

Strive to make your discussions objective so that the reality of a situation has a chance to become clear, rather than being clouded by personal disagreements, hardened positions, or biases.

SITE-BASED MANAGEMENT WORKS FOR PRINCIPALS AND SUPERINTENDENTS

In 1993 Massachusetts passed an educational reform law endorsing site-based management of schools. The law states that "It shall be the responsibility of the principal in consultation with professional staff of the building to promote participatory decision making among all professional staff for the purpose of developing educational policy." This was a very good idea, because improving education from the top down doesn't work. Top-down decisions bypass input from the very people who should be most involved—those who will be doing the *implementing*.

Under site-based management—which is taken even further by our collaborative approach—it is important to consider how to coordinate the roles of leaders at the school level (e.g., principals) and leaders at the district level (e.g., superintendents).

At the school level, in our process, the principal facilitates the improvement of culture and curriculum. Teacher leaders provide leadership with their peers and with parents. All teachers help give shape to improvement plans. As much as is possible, a school's principal and faculty should be allowed to identify and pursue the goals they believe will most improve their school. Who knows the school better than those who are working on a daily basis with its students?

It is the responsibility of every school to transform itself from within.

The superintendent's active support for site-based management is essential. District leadership, in our view, should be in an oversight, advisory, and support role to see that improvement is well-conceived and is progressing at each school. *The superintendent of schools in this way becomes a true leader of leaders.* From our viewpoint, this type of administrative structure best expedites a district's school-by-school transformation.

We see pursuing answers to the following questions as the domain of school district leadership.

- Do we have excellent leadership in each building?
- Does each school have a sound process for improvement?
- Is each school systematically building excellence into their curriculum?
- Are the principals and teacher-leaders trained to run a collaborative process?
- Has each school agreed to a set of working values?

- Are the schools selecting and implementing annual or biennial goals?
- Do the goals offer the greatest positive benefits for students?
- Do the goals follow an educationally sound progression designed to lift student achievement?
- Is there a good level of consistency, coordination and cooperation between schools?
- Are there sufficient opportunities for collaboration, communication, and sharing within and between schools?
- Is performance being measured?
- How are we performing in testing? Are adjustments in test preparation needed? What does the data show? Are the schools making progress?
- Have we built strong remedial processes for those students who might otherwise fall behind?
- What support do the schools need to be successful?
- Is the superintendent monitoring school leadership processes and mentoring the school's administrators?
- Are school leaders abreast of the latest research and development?
- Do the schools need support or training in instruction, curriculum development, classroom management skills, or in other key areas?

Good oversight by the district is essential to protecting the interest of students (e.g., in cases where, for whatever reason, adequate structures are not in place, or there is an unacceptable level of discord between principal and faculty, or there is too much divergence between the schools in their curriculum or preparation of students).

Care must be taken as well not to layer on district, or voluntary state or federal goals, that make it more difficult for the school to continue to move at a good speed in implementing their own school transformation process.

A REVIEW OF CHAPTER 3 CONCEPTS

- A collaborative leader is guided by a strong inner vision and a desire to interact with staff in a manner that builds trust and mutual respect.
- An effective leader strives to lead his or her school at the "vision level."
- The leader's job is to keep the spotlight on striving for operational excellence.
- Schools can unite around making a difference for students.
- The best interest of students has to be the leader's primary motivation if it is to be the school's top priority.
- Improvement requires allocation of time in the regular operating schedule to be taken seriously.

- The limited time and resources for improvement should be spent on goals that are worthy of everyone's time.
- Superior results are achieved not by contending with negatives but by building greater positives.
- An outstanding organization needs to be both highly empowered and highly aligned.
- Agreeing to a set of process steps at the start of goal planning increases the likelihood of a successful result.
- As planning dialogues expand, the presenting group should avoid selling its ideas or conclusions, but should instead present facts and options as a starting point for the next level of discussion.
- A process that stays objective for as long as possible greatly enhances the opportunity for the group to reach the best solution.
- School leaders and faculty should advocate for the opportunity to be guided as much as possible by collaborative site-based management from within.
- The superintendent and central office play an essential role in supporting, coordinating, and overseeing each school's improvement process.

Chapter Four

Developing Outstanding Teamwork

We hope the preceding chapters have provided you with a sense of mission and an overall conceptual background. The next three chapters, "Developing Outstanding Teamwork" (chapter 4), "Uniting Behind a Shared Vision and Focused Goals" (chapter 5), and "Building Cycles of Success" (chapter 6) are concerned with the "how to" practicalities of establishing your collaborative improvement process.

In each of these "how to" chapters, we first address "mindset" issues, followed by a presentation of the process steps. Even after the preceding three chapters of conceptual background, we continue to provide you with mental preparation concepts. *Why?—because the leader's mindset is just as important as the steps being implemented.* Our intent is for you to understand the thinking behind the process. Doing so will maximize the likelihood of your achieving success despite the inevitable unforeseen circumstances and unexpected problems that you may encounter.

TWELVE GUIDELINES FOR THE "HOW TO" PHASES

1. *"Felt-need" Is Always First.* Let's start by focusing on the importance of "felt-need." At the start of the process, we are beginning to move an assemblage of individuals toward thinking and acting like a team. The coalition we are seeking to forge is in an initial tenuous period. It is essential that we begin by helping staff believe in the process.

Felt-need will have been achieved when a critical mass of our employees reaches the conclusion that using teamwork to collaboratively set and achieve focused goals is worth trying. Getting started doesn't require that everyone come to this conclusion—just enough of a critical mass to get us going—let's say 55 to 60 percent of our faculty (although an even higher percentage is desirable).

Given the typical default distribution of staff attitudes, reaching this level of support would mean getting most of the "gung-hos" (25 percent), a slight majority of the "go-with-the-flows" (30 percent), and a few of the "you-can't-do-its" (5 percent). The need to establish this critical mass, along with the general fragility of the presuccess phase, underscores the importance of being especially careful in planning the start of an improvement process. You may only get one chance.

Before attaining "felt-need," any effort to engage staff in implementing the improvement process will produce minimal or no results. Who among us does with enthusiasm something we don't understand or believe in? Until felt-need is attained, however long it takes, there is no point in proceeding.

Initial felt-need doesn't have to reflect a rabid commitment, just 55–60 percent of your staff saying, "OK, let's give this a try." When you get to that level of support, get going.

2. *There is no motivator like success.* If we want our staff to own the organization's problems and to invest themselves in making the organization a success, we must allow them to become true participants—the greater their participation, the greater their ownership.

Initial ownership is based on hope; that will get us to a certain point, but before long, the group needs to experience success in improving some aspect of the school. There is no better way to motivate people than for them to achieve something meaningful.

People will naturally want to experience that success again. If successes are repeated, the group will almost universally come to believe in their ability to work together and to produce positive results.

In the normal course of events, it takes some kind of "emergency situation" for people to put aside their individual issues and really pull together. Teamwork is spontaneously created in these situations. People know they must work together and depend on one another. There is instant camaraderie caused by the event. We saw this in the rapid response by diverse parties to the incredible landing of Captain Sullenberger's U.S. Airways flight in the Hudson River, and more recently in response to the Boston Marathon bombing. People do great things when they put aside differences and work together.

That brings us to these two questions: (1) How do we pull people together *not* under emergency circumstances; and (2) How do we *keep people working together* long enough to secure some motivating successes? *At the start we want you to be very aware that your initial mission is to get people together and keep them together until they experience a success or two.* At that point, energy will start to flow from those successes.

3. *Build from where people are.* Don't ask your staff to make any huge leaps of faith. It will be difficult enough to engage them to a point of critical mass so you can get going—anything that stretches them too much at the start will cause apprehension and feed negative points of view. Don't rush it; incremental progress is fine. Think of stairs as a metaphor—one little step doesn't seem like much, but after a number of them you've moved higher up, and without stress.

4. *Everyone needs to feel protected.* The initial steps should contain reassurances that overcome skepticism or presumptions of insincerity. Put safeguards in place to assure participants that the improvement process will be nothing but what it seems—open, honest, and in their control. An example of such a reassurance might be for the leader to remind the staff that each of the process steps and other key decisions will be subject to the consensus of the group.

5. *Violations of trust are death to the process.* Those leading the process should attentively avoid violations of trust, or anything that even *appears* to be damaging to trust. These infractions include behaviors such as not listening, pushing your ideas, rigging outcomes, lobbying for votes outside of an open meeting, talking about others behind their backs, and all the other "opposites" of the working values.

6. *Consensus is a great protection.* Explaining consensus will reassure the group. Consensus, as we conceive it, means that time has been provided for the issues to be fully discussed, the plusses and minuses have been fully explored, everyone has had an opportunity to weigh in, and we have worked hard for 100 percent support. In instances when differences can't be fully reconciled and a vote is necessary, we feel there still needs to be a minimum of 75 percent in favor of going ahead. While this percentage is somewhat arbitrary on our part, we are certain of one thing: *The percentage of the group that gets behind a decision needs to be high.*

Recall that we said the initial critical mass to begin the process is about 55–60 percent. That percentage reflects the practicality of merely beginning—we are saying as a group, "Let's try this, it could be good for our school." Once we start putting the process together and making decisions, once we start changing things in the school, the percentage of support needs to move up to 75 percent and above. Do not leave substantial minorities behind.

7. *Trust the ability of the group.* Put your mind at ease about the group's ability to choose wisely. If a group has a good process to follow, one that focuses criteria for decision making on what is best for students, one that looks for the most important areas for improvement, and one that considers options thoroughly and objectively, they will make good decisions.

8. *Agree on process steps.* If process steps are not agreed upon through completion of a task, an opening is created that could allow the process to go

astray. However, going too far ahead at any one time can be overwhelming and scare people. Balance the need to know where we are going without projecting too far into the future. That is why we recommend installing our collaborative improvement process in four phases:

- *Phase I:* proceeding with a collaborative improvement process (in this chapter);
- *Phase II:* structuring improved professional relationships—creating the "working values" (in this chapter);
- *Phase III:* the steps to obtain a vision, set focused goals, form teams, and articulate objectives and action plans (chapter 5);
- *Phase IV:* the steps that establish a renewable improvement process (chapter 6).

9. *Maintain a "winning attitude" at all times.* What we call a "winning attitude" begins by keeping the end in mind. What do we want to see three to five years out? A typical positive vision would be for *everyone in the school* to be working together smoothly, creating effective new educational systems for our school. If that is the end we seek—everyone working together productively—it is important not to act in any way in the present that might prevent that future from happening. Don't write people off. Don't get involved in power struggles or burn any bridges. Over time just about everyone will gradually come on board as you begin to experience success.

10. *Don't require, inspire.* This doesn't mean that you won't require attendance at faculty meetings—or that when people accept responsibility for something we won't hold them accountable—or that we will accept passive sabotage. We still have to manage and supervise; however, our primary motivation is *inspired* not "ordered." Our source of motivation, enthusiasm, and optimism comes from the joy and satisfaction of working together and successfully producing great results for our students.

11. *Establish a culture of encouragement.* We want a culture in our school characterized by support and encouragement. Most people who will help the school achieve success do not do so for the recognition. However, when they are recognized for what they do, it does make them feel good and it sets a standard for others.

Studies over the years have shown that in classrooms, homes, and workplaces a positive, successful environment is established when encouraging comments and supportive words or actions outweigh corrective words or actions by a ratio of 3:1 or 4:1.

We first read about the 4 to 1 rule in the 1990s in an excellent book entitled *Bringing Out the Best in People* by Dr. Aubrey Daniels. More recently the Harvard Business Review Blog spread the word that the standard ought to be even higher, when it brought attention to a most interesting study by Marcial Losada and Emily Heaphy, "The Role of Positivity and Connectivity in the Performance of Business Teams" (originally reported in the *American Behavioral Scientist* Journal in 2004). That study found that 5 to 1 was even better.

What is so interesting was the finding *that work performance on employee teams paralleled the level of support—the interpersonal atmosphere—on the team.* The highest performing teams encouraged each other 5 to 1 (positive to negative comments). Medium performing teams reinforced on average 1.9 to1, and the lowest performing teams had a 1 to 3 ratio in the negative. These results speak volumes about the value of creating a supportive environment.

This rationale is all about noticing when people are doing first-rate work and providing recognition. One variation on this theme is to include a "thank you time" in meeting agendas, allowing a few minutes for people to freely compliment each other for effort and supportive behavior. The compliments will powerfully demonstrate that acts of kindness, generosity, and extra effort are noticed and appreciated.

Joe: "I have had the experience of receiving appreciative comments at a meeting. The most amazing thing to me is how people remembered me saying or doing something supportive *that I had completely forgotten.* These actions meant so much to the person at the time that they did not forget. It is a compelling lesson for everyone to hear how people appreciate and remember instances of encouragement and support. It shows us that seemingly small acts make a difference."

12. *Changing the culture changes the people.* The processes in this book will change people, at least in their working environment, and often beyond. Believing in your colleagues and believing in oneself feels very different inside compared to fear, insecurity, mistrust, doubt, and low expectations. When we contribute in a leadership capacity (as many in the process will) and see the benefits to our school, we are changed. When our new positive feelings become entrenched, we are permanently changed.

INSTALLING THE PROCESS

We've divided the installation of the process into four phases. Here, in chapter 4, we concentrate on the steps of Phase I, reaching agreement to move forward with the process, and the steps of Phase II, improving professional relationships.

Ready to start?—Here we go!

PHASE I: STEPS THAT TAKE US THROUGH THE DECISION TO PROCEED WITH A COLLABORATIVE IMPROVEMENT PROCESS

In the remainder of this chapter we will discuss the first two phases of the improvement process. We want to caution you against the natural tendency to think, "To heck with this list of things, let's just work together and get some good stuff done." If you follow the steps we suggest in this book, you are setting up a system that will still be working smoothly ten years and more from now. If what you build is going to last, it is important that it be done in a way that lays down a solid foundation. Keep in mind during each of the Phase I steps that you are in the most tenuous stage of the process. Plan well and take your time, but don't be tenuous yourself—be confident and upbeat.

Below, we list the *Phase I process steps* in abbreviated form, followed by a discussion of each in more detail.

1. Meet informally with a prospective coordinating team of six to eight teachers.
2. Establish felt-need within the coordinating team.
3. Briefly outline the process.
4. Alert your school council.
5. Meet a second time with the coordinating team and agree to proceed.
6. Schedule a series of faculty meetings.
7. Establish felt-need at the first faculty meeting.
8. Conduct a series of meetings and exercises with the faculty.
9. Discuss and reach agreement about proceeding with a collaborative improvement process.
10. If the faculty chooses to proceed, then engage the other stakeholders.

Phase I, Step 1: Meet informally with a prospective coordinating team of six to eight teachers. Select six to eight teachers who are respected by the faculty and who represent a cross-section of positive faculty groups, friendships, grades, and subjects. Eight is a good number. You are looking for potentially supportive people from the "gung-hos" and the "go-with-the-flows." We suggest not engaging the hard core "you-can't-do-its" until you start building momentum. The idea is to begin with teachers who are generally representative of, and well respected by, the faculty—a group that will tend to give new ideas a fair hearing, but that will also provide you with some objective feedback.

Phase I, Step 2: Establish felt-need within the coordinating team. Share with the coordinating team that as you see it, your job has two main components—a management component to ensure smooth daily operations, and a leadership component that is more long term and goal oriented. Tell them that while the management responsibilities are certainly important and require constant attentiveness, the leadership side of the ledger is in some ways more challenging—especially for just one person to take on.

Inform the team that you believe the leadership component would benefit from an increase in staff collaboration, so that key priority decisions about how to improve the school are more reflective of a wider range of views. Engage the group in one or more of the *Opening Exercises* found in appendix C. Explain your interest in pursuing collaborative improvement. Avoid pushing too hard, but do allow your sincerity and genuine interest in exploring these concepts to show.

Phase I, Step 3: Briefly outline the process. Do your best to summarize the key elements of the process for the coordinating team, including these Phase I steps; refer to sections of the preface and conclusion. The main point is to emphasize that the process will allow you to improve working relationships and to share improvement planning with the faculty by selecting and working together on a series of improvement goals and objectives.

Share your interest and enthusiasm with the group. Tell them the process makes sense to you, and explain that you are interested in their input. Consider giving out copies of the book and asking the coordinating team to read it, focusing for now on the first three chapters. Schedule a second meeting in a week or two.

Phase I, Step 4: Alert your school council. Tell the school council, as an informational "heads up," that you will be discussing a process for collaborative improvement planning with the faculty; inform them that if the faculty is interested you will put the subject on a council agenda. Pass out copies of an introductory handout, or ask the school council to read the book's first three chapters.

Phase I, Step 5: Meet a second time with the coordinating team and agree to proceed. Discuss using a collaborative improvement process in your school. See if they want to proceed with the first phase. You can be honest and present it as something you are very interested in, but don't "push it hard." Avoid the "you sell, they respond" dynamic—that approach could be seen as manipulative, and hence the natural inclination would be to say "no."

Ask the group to share their thoughts about such a process with each other and with you. Go around the group. This meeting should be an open discussion of the process and what it has to offer your school. *Could this be good for our school?* When all thoughts are out on the table, ask the coordinating team if they wish to proceed, explaining that the next step would be to expand the discussion to the full faculty. Talk through any questions or concerns the group has and reach a good consensus before moving on. If they require additional meetings, that's OK. Moving on without felt-need is a mistake.

Phase I, Step 6: Schedule a series of faculty meetings. Work with the coordinating team to plan a series of faculty meetings—or a half- or full-day session if that works best. Involve them in the preparation and planning of the meetings. Let them recruit any additional persons whose participation as presenters they feel would be helpful. Circulate copies of an introductory handout or the book to teachers who express an interest.

Phase I, Step 7: Establish felt-need at the first faculty meeting. Always make establishing felt-need your highest priority with any new group that enters the expanding discussion. In this case, you are going from the coordinating team to the full faculty. Felt-need is the most essential ingredient in building critical mass to the requisite 55–60 percent level. Again, be honest, sincere, and optimistic.

Open the meeting by sharing the same types of thoughts as you did with the smaller coordinating group. Provide an overview of the process. Let the coordinating team share their thoughts with the faculty. Involve them in a meaningful way in the presentation so the proposed initiative doesn't seem to be coming only from you, but from you as leader *jointly with* the coordinating team. Felt-need is all about catching the vision—in this case, the initial vision that *the process could be good for the school.*

Phase I, Step 8: Conduct a series of meetings and exercises with the faculty. Lead the faculty through some of the exercises described in appendixes C and F. Read through them yourself and select those you feel would be most effective in demonstrating to your staff the value of engaging in a collaborative improvement process. The exercises are intended as part of building felt-need; they are tools meant to clarify the worth of the process.

Involve the coordinating team as much as possible. (Start building leaders for the process right from the beginning.) Even if you are short of time for this phase, make sure that you get to the "Best Workplace" exercise (appendix C) as well as the "If Things Went Great" exercise (appendix F). They should not be skipped, because they are essential to establishing group motivation and felt-need.

Phase I, Step 9: Discuss and reach agreement about proceeding with a collaborative improvement process. Always try to conclude a work session so that everyone clearly sees a result for his or her efforts. Do not have a great discussion and then conclude vaguely. Always recap what you did and talk about what's next. After the exercises, it is time to ask the faculty if they would like to proceed with establishing a collaborative process for planning school improvements. Explain that they are giving themselves permission to participate in improvement planning and *accepting your proposal to share improvement-planning decisions with them.*

Assure them again that nothing will be planned or decided without their participation, and that group consensus will control the direction and pace of the process. Explain that you feel involving the faculty as decision-making partners in improvement planning gives them a real voice in the future of the school. Offer to find meeting time for the process by using e-mail or intranet/

website postings for more routine administrative matters so that some improvement work can occur during time already set aside for meetings.

Ask the coordinating team to remind the group that the key elements being offered are

1. to reach agreements to improve professional working relationships so that our school begins to approximate the characteristics of a "best workplace" environment, and
2. to focus our efforts at improving the school by pursuing a vision and an associated limited number of goals at any one time—goals that we will choose together—thus allowing us to move forward together in a couple of priority directions instead of ineffectually pursuing many directions at once.

For this discussion, try to avoid a model where the faculty poses questions and the leader answers them. This creates an " us and them " mental divide that can easily turn into separation.

Allow the coordinating team and the teachers as a group to respond to questions. Turn questions to you into questions for them. "Does this approach make sense to you?" "What do you see as the pros and cons?" *The discussion is then centered on whether or not such a plan makes sense, the pros and cons of it, and is not about responding to the "principal's plan."* If you sense the need to come back for additional meeting(s) to build more understanding and support, do so. Keep in mind that you must establish felt-need. Don't rush it—remain respectful, patient, and calm. Remember that you are initiating a long-term process.

Phase I, Step 10: If the faculty chooses to proceed, then engage the other stakeholders. Conduct a similar abbreviated process with the school council if you have one. In Massachusetts, the councils are composed of the principal, teachers, parents, and sometimes a community member or two. They are primarily concerned with the direction of the school and the school improvement plan, so they are important to the process. Ask faculty members on the council to help you with the planning and presentation. Include members of the coordinating team if you sense that is appropriate. Engage the council in a discussion leading to their support. If the council raises any serious concerns, bring them back to the faculty.

Streamline the process with other groups such as nonfaculty staff and parents. Engage them in similar discussions and seek their support for the faculty's decision to proceed. If any of the stakeholder groups raise an issue, be sure to bring it back to the faculty and make every effort to reconcile differences. All stakeholders must know that the concerns they express are taken seriously in order for them to feel real ownership of the improvement process. That will naturally occur if you record, discuss, and faithfully work your way through any questions or problems that arise.

Let's add a little information here about our rationale for sequencing discussions. We prefer to have the faculty and principal meet first and provide their input to the school council, nonfaculty staff, and parent representative groups. The other stakeholder groups will want to know what the faculty and principal think, so it makes sense for the faculty and principal to go first. Any suggestions made thereafter by the school council, nonfaculty staff, or parents are brought back to the faculty and principal, who are always part of the final negotiation and agreement.

The faculty and principal need to be at the center of the decision-making process from beginning to end, because they are the ones closest to the students, most knowledgeable about the educational program, and most responsible for implementation of any changes. They make the planned improvements come alive in the classroom; therefore, they need to be enthusiastically supportive of any plans created.

On occasion, when considering vision or mission statements or setting other longer-term planning goals, the principal can conduct a joint meeting of representatives from the faculty, nonfaculty staff, school council, and parents (each prepared with input and priorities from their respective groups). Such a conclave may be used to decide broad, long-term policy. Ask each group to come to the meeting prepared to share their top three improvement goals for the school. You can then determine if those can be combined into a broad vision and goals.

If the principal or the faculty have concerns about something decided by a meeting of the representatives from all groups, bring those concerns to the representative body and negotiate a resolution that allows everyone to get on board.

You will have completed this phase when all groups have given the process a green light.

PHASE II: STEPS TO IMPROVE PROFESSIONAL RELATIONSHIPS: CREATING THE "WORKING VALUES"

Assuming that the stakeholders all agree to move forward, we proceed to the second phase of process steps. This phase primarily *involves establishing professional agreements to support outstanding teamwork*. The centerpiece is the *working values*.

The *Phase II process steps* are listed below and then addressed in more detail.

1. Select or retain a coordinating team.

2. Train the coordinating team in the effective meeting process.
3. With the coordinating team, schedule three or four faculty meetings.
4. With the coordinating team, consider the use of "preliminary" discussion questions.
5. Provide the full faculty with a packet containing "A Guide to Effective Meetings"; "A Guide to Consensus"; the results of the "Best Workplace" and "If Things Went Great" exercises from Phase I; and a copy of the one-page "Working Values."
6. At a series of faculty meetings, first discuss the "Guide to Effective Meetings" and the "Guide to Consensus"; then the outcomes from the "Best Workplace" and "If Things Went Great" exercises; then discuss preliminary questions if any; last of all, introduce the "Working Values."
7. Resolve issues at meetings by working toward consensus.
8. Enlist the coordinating team to draft language for suggested changes in the working values as needed.
9. Meet again with the full faculty and vote on the working values or any other professional agreements.
10. Ask the school council, nonfaculty staff, and parent groups to review and discuss the effective meeting guidelines, consensus, and the working values chosen by the faculty.
11. Reconcile differences and reach consensus with all stakeholder groups on the working values.
12. Finalize the working values and ask all groups to adopt, distribute, and post them.

Phase II, Step 1: Select or retain a coordinating team. Eight is a good number for the coordinating team in this phase. For the sake of continuity, it is helpful if at least some of the members who assisted with the first phase want to continue, but now that the whole faculty has committed to the process, you could ask the faculty to select eight members instead of you selecting them. Our preferred alternative would be to see how many phase-one members want to continue, and then add new members who wish to volunteer.

You can avoid a selection or election by expanding the size of the team if there are additional teachers who want to serve. It is best for the process to allow members to stay on if they wish, while asking whether others would like to join. In a process that depends on motivation don't discourage volunteers and don't appear to have a closed shop.

Later, when you move on to goal setting in Phase III, the members of the coordinating team will be excellent candidates to provide leadership for the planning teams that will be formed around specific goals. They will already be schooled in the process and will be able to help those planning teams get off to a good start.

Phase II, Step 2: Train the coordinating team in the effective meeting process. At your first opportunity, train the team in the "effective meeting process" (appendix A) and also discuss the material on consensus (appendix B).

The greatest asset of teamwork can also be its greatest drawback—there are a lot of people involved and a lot of viewpoints to mold into a consensus. If we smoothly tap into the extensive knowledge base of our employees, and keep the process moving forward to maintain enthusiasm and momentum, teamwork can't be beat in its productivity. On the other hand, if meetings are poorly planned, argumentative in style, scattered in focus, and easily bogged down, the collaborative improvement process will fail. The quality of meetings is important.

We offer you our guidelines for conducting effective meetings and reaching consensus; but whether you use them or choose your own meeting guidelines, make sure that participants leave your meetings without frustration and with a sense of accomplishment.

Phase II, Step 3: With the coordinating team, schedule three or four faculty meetings. The number of meetings depends on the group and the issues that might come up, so it's hard to predict how many you'll need. *Make the point that each phase must take as long as it takes to do it well.* If the leader and the coordinating team see the group productively working through issues, let them have the time. If the group is going over the same ground repeatedly, then bring things to a head and move along.

Laying in a good foundation takes time, but don't do it so slowly that people lose interest.

Phase II, Step 4: With the coordinating team, consider the use of "preliminary" discussion questions.

Ken: "There is no substitute for knowing your staff and how ready they are. I knew there were substantial relationship issues at the start of the Doyon School's process. It took almost a full year to establish the type of professional relationships that would support our efforts to work together as a 'team.' We used the following preliminary sets of questions to get there: *(1) Why are you here? What brought you into education? (2) What is it you need from the rest of the staff? What kind of support do we want to receive from each other? (3) What do we want to include in a set of working values?*"

If you feel that you need to build your staff's empathy and esteem, plan to use some or all of these questions as discussion starters during the faculty meetings. They are almost always worthwhile as a precursor to discussing the working values.

Phase II, Step 5: Provide the full faculty with a packet containing " A Guide to Effective Meetings" (appendix A); "A Guide to Consensus" (appen-

dix B); the results of the "Best Workplace" and "If Things Went Great" exercises from Phase I; and a copy of the one-page "Working Values" (appendix D). Add any other information that you want your teachers to consider in advance of the series of full faculty meetings.

Phase II, Step 6: At a series of faculty meetings, first discuss the "Guide to Effective Meetings" and the "Guide to Consensus"; then the outcomes from the "Best Workplace" and "If Things Went Great" exercises; then discuss preliminary questions if any; last of all, introduce the "Working Values." For each full faculty meeting provide an agenda.

Consider using the Roundtable format for the discussion of preliminary questions (see exercise #1 in appendix G). Go around the group, giving everyone a chance to speak. Go around more than once if you have the time. Post the responses in short phrases. Distill and develop a list of key points. Add these to the list of outcomes from the "Best Workplace" and "If Things Went Great" exercises. Compare the collective list of outcomes from discussions and exercises to the starter list of working values in appendix D. Use this comparison as a source for potentially creating additional working values.

This step involves a number of sessions. Take your time. It is not a race. Make as much progress as you can while letting people have the opportunity to speak. Remember you are modeling an inclusive process but you also want to keep things moving along.

We model an inclusive, collaborative process by providing attendees the opportunity to speak, and by being attentive and interested in what they say. Follow lines of thought; ask questions to obtain deeper clarity; allow speakers to make their point fully.

Phase II, Step 7: Resolve issues at meetings by working toward consensus. How to reach consensus is a point of critical understanding. We've already touched upon aspects of consensus earlier in this chapter, and we provide an overview in appendix B. You will find additional comments on consensus in chapter 5. We give consensus this kind of emphasis because the ability to achieve consensus lies at the heart of resolving difficult issues as a group. *We must be able to conclude issues in order to stay united while moving forward.*

Phase II, Step 8: Enlist the coordinating team to draft language for suggested changes in the working values as needed. Drafting language is a difficult and poor use of time with a large group. Better to get ideas on the table and then delegate the actual writing to a smaller drafting group that can perfect language or sort out options.

Don't take up the time of the full faculty drafting language or researching. Faculty meeting time should be used primarily for evaluating options and making decisions.

The task of drafting should go to the coordinating team or a subgroup of writing specialists. The assigned persons should take particularly good notes and cross-check them with the meeting notetaker. (Right from the start, seek volunteers to fill the roles called for in the effective meeting process.) It is essential that the members of the drafting team were present at the related faculty meetings so they understand context, intonation, and the reasoning behind particular ideas.

When the drafting group presents options to the faculty, it is again an "expanded dialogue starting point," offered with the understanding and expectation that the faculty is likely to make changes and edits. Don't fall in love with your draft. Instead, understand that when the faculty finishes it will be even better.

The job of the drafting group is to save everyone else a lot of time by taking a first "try" at the task, thus allowing the larger group to begin from an advanced starting point.

Ken: "The very first time we reached the stage of asking a drafting team to meet between meetings and to report back to the full group, a veteran faculty member announced with some vehemence, *'This group isn't going to meet without me.'* This particular teacher didn't usually volunteer for committees and I was a bit taken aback. After a few moments, I understood: She was insisting on being a part of the group because of her apprehension that the work of the drafting group would become the *final* version or very close to it, and would be presented to the full staff as a fait accompli.

"While I had clearly defined the limited mission of the drafting group, the teacher did not trust my words. I didn't think further assurances would do much good, so I welcomed her on board. Because we had two different drafting groups working on separate tasks, I even arranged for them to meet at different times so she could be a participant in both.

"It is important to keep in mind the doubt and cynicism that members of your staff will inevitably have internalized because of past experiences. This negativity is a hurdle to overcome, but faithful implementation of the process—and a successful improvement cycle—will eliminate most of it. After the above incident, in the many years of ongoing improvement work, there was never any further insinuation of distrust by this teacher or any other staff member regarding the defined responsibilities of a drafting group.

"Everyone knew that the work of such teams was only the starting point to open the larger group discussion, and that all discussions would be open and transparent without hidden agendas or prior lobbying."

Phase II, Step 9: Meet again with the full faculty and vote on the working values or any other professional agreements. The working values as discussed in chapter 2 speak for themselves. Other areas of professional agreement could cover a variety of topics that the group might or might not wish to incorporate in a statement of working values. You might consider, for example, agreeing upon some of these types of procedural or relational issues:

- attending all meetings;
- being prompt for meetings;
- always having a written agenda;
- honoring meeting times by starting and ending promptly;
- extending daily greetings to others;
- being supportive and complimentary whenever possible; and
- supporting ideas enthusiastically after consensus.

The first four items above are potential meeting guidelines; the last three are candidates for a professional agreement or inclusion in the working values. The steps are to discuss them fully, to come to consensus, and to put anything important to good process in writing.

Phase II, Step 10: Ask the school council, nonfaculty staff, and parent groups to review and discuss the effective meeting guidelines, consensus, and the working values chosen by the faculty. On a broad, major issue like the working values (or the school vision), what the faculty and principal decide should be passed on to the school council, nonfaculty staff as a group, and to a representative group of parents. The views of all stakeholders should be reconciled via discussions leading to consensus. However, keep in mind that the faculty and the principal should not be forced to accept a value or goal for which they have an objection.

If achieving an objective requires nonfaculty staff or parents to play a *direct role*, such as a new homework policy involving parents, or policies regarding staff interaction with students concerning discipline or bullying, then that group should be a part of the discussion and decision.

Be sure the following key aspects of the decision-making process are clear to everyone.

1. The primary purpose of the collaborative improvement process is *improvement planning, not management*; the latter will be done via the usual chain of command.
2. The components of the improvement process with the broadest scope like mission, vision, and working values should be decided by the broadest group of stakeholders, while annual goals, objectives, and action plans should be decided primarily by the principal, faculty, and council with periodic input from nonfaculty staff and parents.
3. The guideline that overrides all others with regard to who participates in decision making is as follows: *The parties who are needed to implement an improvement should be participants in planning that improvement.*

Ken: "The Massachusetts Education Reform Act of 1993, which mandated school councils, was passed two years before I began to work with Joe and Nels. The law requires councils to prepare an annual 'school improvement plan' to identify improvement goals for the year. For several years I dutifully worked to prepare those plans with the five parents, five staff members, and community representatives who were on the council. These early plans were exceedingly well written, thoughtful, and ambitious—*but had little or no impact on the school.*

Each year when the plan was presented to the faculty, as much as I cajoled and tried to convince, and as enthusiastic as I was personally, what consistently emerged was support from some, objections from others, and indifference from the rest. I just couldn't get everyone on the same page; hence, no substantial improvement occurred. In fact, there were times when the plans led to divisiveness and made the school climate worse.

The lesson learned is this: If you want to maximize your faculty getting 'on board,' begin the process with them, extend the discussion to other groups, then bring their ideas back to the faculty. While in the end you need consensus and agreement between the groups, by positioning the principal and faculty as the hub around which improvement discussions revolve, you will maximize their engagement."

Phase II, Step 11: Reconcile differences and reach consensus with all stakeholder groups on the working values. All groups should agree to the same set of working values. They should be your school's working values, the same for everyone. Any differences or suggested additions should be discussed and reconciled. Only values agreed to by all should be on the list.

The working values can be used creatively, for instance, by applying them to interactions with parents bringing problems to school for resolution. Other groups, visitors, vendors, etc., should also be asked to abide by the school's working values while interacting in discussions and meetings with school personnel.

Broad use of the working values will help to tone down situations when persons from outside of school interject less than productive problem-solving styles (which might rely on dramatics, abrasive behaviors, or personal attacks) in their communication with the school. The working values can steer the discussion toward the real issues and increase the likelihood of a positive resolution for the child. When parents or others come to the school with a problem, give them a copy of the working values prior to beginning a discussion of the issues. Tell them that we want to reach a resolution most beneficial to the child, so we need to proceed on a basis that will produce the best results. *In our house, the house rules apply.*

Phase II, Step 12: Finalize the working values and ask all groups to adopt, distribute, and post them. Ask all groups to formally adopt the working values and to live by them. Distribute copies to all members, and post them in all classrooms, offices, and public locations. Find an appropriate occasion at least once a year to have people take turns reading them aloud at a staff meeting. Revisit them for changes every couple of years. Take them seriously; keep them alive.

The working values represent your staff's highest aspirations for who they would like to be in their working relationships with each other; they call your entire organization up to a higher standard of professional interaction.

DO NOT LET THE NUMBER OF STEPS CONCERN YOU

Ken: "We've broken the steps down so that they are inclusive and detailed. We wanted you to have a very thorough process available to you, with no steps missing. This we believe will maximize the likelihood of your successfully accomplishing the installation of the process without damaging missteps. In actual practice, many of the steps are not lengthy at all.

"At the risk of being redundant, I'm going to restate a caution here: If you were to say, 'I'm just going to go ahead and talk with my staff and make some common-sense changes for the better,' you would be leading in the unsuccessful style I used before we created this process.

"*Transformation—deep-seated change—requires the creation of new patterns and realities. New realities are not created easily; the work of transformation must be done carefully and wisely. As Deming often said, 'It is not instant pudding.' It takes time.*"

A REVIEW OF CHAPTER 4 CONCEPTS

- Before asking people to act, establish "felt-need."
- Use the exercises in appendixes C and F to help create felt-need; be sure to include the "Best Workplace" and "If Things Went Great" exercises.
- There is no better way to motivate a group in the long term than for them to experience success together.
- Caught inspiration is your most powerful weapon—it comes from working and succeeding together.
- Build from where people are. Don't ask for huge leaps of faith.
- Everyone needs to feel protected. Provide assurances that the collaborative process will be open, transparent, and in the control of the group.
- The dialogue to embrace collaboration moves from the principal, to the coordinating team, to the faculty, to the other stakeholders.
- The principal and faculty are the hub of the process; it begins and ends with them.

- Initial critical mass means a 55 percent plurality or better. Decisions about the school's future call for a 75 percent plurality or better—preferably consensus agreement.
- Consensus is a great protection; be sure everyone understands what it is.
- Train the coordinating team, faculty, and school council in effective meetings and consensus.
- In a culture of encouragement, we notice and name the good things people do; seek a culture characterized by a 4:1 or 5:1 ratio of support over corrections.
- Create and rely on a set of working values to elevate the working culture; then keep the working values alive.
- Use the working values with parents and others who come to school for problem resolution.
- The creation of new realities is not easy; it takes time.
- Take the time to do things well, but not so slowly that people lose interest.

Chapter Five

Uniting Behind a Shared Vision and Focused Goals

TURNING YOUR SCHOOL INTO A POWERFUL POSITIVE FORCE

This chapter is about transforming your school into a *powerful force* for improvement and accomplishment by cultivating, harnessing, focusing, and then releasing the energy within your staff.

The normal state of affairs in an organization is not "vision," but "division." Without a coalescing vision, the various parties to an enterprise operate from their own comfort zones, predispositions, and individual egos.

Individuals will step outside of their comfort zones and predispositions for the benefit of the school—*if they are inspired by a vision and a set of goals.* Inspiration began to build when your staff became more closely in touch with their ideals, had the experience of sharing those thoughts with each other in the various discussions and exercises, and agreed to interact at a higher professional level through the adoption of working values.

Hope has been kindled, but that is not enough to fully unite them. They need to arrive at a point where they can reflect on an achievement and think, "That was a really good accomplishment for our school, and we made it happen." That type of positive accomplishment will make them want to duplicate the experience, particularly if their collaboration was enjoyable and they celebrated what they achieved. *Accomplishment is the glue that binds successful organizations.*

TURNING ON THE SECOND OF THE TWIN ENGINES

We believe that accomplishment runs on "twin engines":

1. The ability of the principal and staff to *work together enthusiastically, respectfully, and productively*, and
2. The ability of the principal and staff to *unite behind and implement a vision and a succession of focused goals and objectives.*

In this chapter you will learn how to "turn on" the second of these "twin engines." Just as the first engine, an upgrade in personal dynamics, culminated in the adoption of a set of working values, the second, a process for formulating a vision and goals, will lead to the drafting of objectives and action strategies in the form of a one-page school improvement plan.

THE ONE-PAGE SCHOOL IMPROVEMENT PLAN

When we started working together, the school improvement plans at the Doyon School were about fifteen pages long. If you asked average teachers what was in the plan they couldn't tell you. We needed something more easily understood and displayed—something that obtained more focus.

Our solution was the one-page improvement plan. We thought to ourselves, "Once the school's goals are focused and limited, what if we put all key components of the improvement plan on a single page in the form of a tree diagram?" We wanted to make it easy for all interested parties to understand the status of the improvement effort.

Familiarizing yourself with this format now will provide a more concrete image of the goal-setting process. As you will see, the plans include vision, mission, goals, objectives, action plans, and timelines—all in a concise format (see appendix E).

SEVEN CONCEPTS TO PREPARE YOU FOR PHASE III:

1. Make your first effort a good one.

Nels: "Despite all the evidence we have right before our eyes, organizations act de facto as if time and resources for improvement were infinite. Organizations tend to have a laundry list of improvement goals. If an idea seems good for the organization, people want it in the plan. Even if all the ideas are worthwhile, which they often are, there are compelling reasons to prioritize the list. As you come to an initial critical mass of support, you will have only so much 'motivational capital.' People will expend effort based on hope and optimism, but the amount of that expenditure is definitely limited. *Hope and optimism are motivators that have a shelf life.*

"Due to the all-consuming nature of day-to-day operations, the amount of time that can be taken away from those tasks to plan improvements is clearly finite. Add to that the tendency of people to get discouraged unless they sense that progress is at least on the horizon. If nothing concrete is accomplished within a reasonable period of time, your staff will soon begin to lose heart and the 'you-can't-do-it' hardcore will have an opening to rebuild their constituency.

"The need to focus our efforts is not an option but a necessity. Make your first initiatives good ones; there may not be a second opportunity. If your staff comes to regard what you are doing as 'another program of the month,' you may not be able to overcome that perception.

"In industry, as in education, the work force has already experienced various management initiatives that reflect the latest popular 'silver bullet.' They get jaded by this succession of 'latest things,' and rightfully so. *There are no silver bullets, in our opinion.* Success is all about the hard work of renewing and revitalizing the operational system piece by piece, step by step. Skeptics and realists are only convinced by accomplishment. Success links the process to people's emotions and gives it real staying power. It is a well-established psychological principle that the reception of some internal benefit (e.g., the emotional impact of helping to produce an achievement you care about) is a necessity for a behavior to be valued and repeated."

Once you have 'achieved together,' the percentage of your staff that buys into the improvement process jumps upward from the level of initial critical mass (55–60 percent based on hope) to substantially higher levels (70–90 percent based on both hope *and* accomplishment). Repeated successes will cause the level of staff engagement to go over 90 percent.

When deciding on goals and objectives, either target achievable near-term milestones within longer-term goals, or, while you are researching longer-term goals, set a shorter, more obtainable goal that might be categorized as "lower-hanging fruit." Do this so your staff can experience a "boost" of success early on while pursuing longer-term objectives. But always work on things that make a difference, even in the short term.

We have found that a discussion of vision, mission, and goals in a school often breaks down naturally into two broad areas for improvement: (1) academics/curriculum, and (2) culture/climate. Within each of these categories, seek to identify areas where relatively quick consensus and accomplishment are possible. For instance, you might want to work on developing rubrics in every classroom that define what constitutes quality work; or it might be time to revise and refine the school's discipline protocols. The idea is to identify areas where success is achievable in a relatively short period (short term defined in months, not years).

It is also possible for a longer-term goal like improving student reading programs to have a relatively shorter-term milestone. The selection of a new reading program and the completion of training in that program are observable milestones short of full implementation. Such milestones provide morale-boosting success while serving as a part of a longer-term goal, particularly if the milestone is celebrated.

Initial achievement is important—your staff needs to see signs of moving toward success to maintain and increase the level of buy-in, and to ensure that enthusiasm doesn't wane.

2. *Passing the Test of Time.* Everything is in a constant state of change. It is the nature of this world that nothing stays the same. If an organization performs well over a long period of time, it is evidence that (a) despite turnover in both leadership and staff, new employees are being properly hired and trained, (b) the culture of the organization continues to inspire the staff, and (c) the organization's strategy is keeping pace with changing times.

If leadership isn't calling your organization up to something higher, it is likely to be descending to something lower.

We don't stand still or drift sideways for long before we start slipping backward. We are either building or unraveling. A focused improvement effort is not a luxury, it's a necessity. If improvement is important to an organization's future, it needs to be given our most precious resource—time.

We can measure commitment to future excellence by whether or not we are setting aside blocks of time in our regular operating schedule dedicated to improvement.

Are we allotting "improvement" an amount of time commensurate with its value? We aren't referring to just an occasional meeting here and there, but rather to ongoing meaningful preset times. The amount of improvement will be commensurate with the time we've committed to it.

3. *The Importance of Our Attitude toward Self, Others, and Life.* To lead a goal-setting and achievement process we need to become "masters of our own thoughts," and focus those thoughts on the targeted outcome of achieving outstanding collaboration.

Self: Be mindful of the nature of your inner conversations—particularly your repeated self-talk. Be careful what you admit into your personal "rumination room." Reject as soon as they raise their ugly heads any repeated thoughts about you that are negative and doubting. If this kind of thinking is an old habit, work to get rid of it and establish a new pattern of reflection on more positive thoughts. It is fine to evaluate, learn from our behavior, and move on. What we ruminate about, what is repeated over and over in our minds, is a different matter in that it is a selection process, so do your best to select something positive to dwell on.

In his book, *Evolve Your Brain,* Dr. Joe Dispenza observes that if we wish to avoid being controlled by our environment, our body, or our emotional responses, we must become better observers of "self."

One of the most powerful things you can do for yourself is to question the thoughts you continuously mull over. Every day good and bad things happen. Positive and negative thoughts are offered to you in your mind. Selecting the negatives (cherry-picking them) for rumination, going over and over them in our mind, mentally chewing on them like a dog on a bone, "primes" us to make exaggerated, negative responses, especially in stressful situations.

Others: Think of a time when you did something you were not very proud of—some really negative behavior on your part. For most of us that poor behavior did not cause us to give up on ourselves. Why? Because when we look at ourselves we see a much greater whole inside of us, with so many other facets to our character that reflect an effort to do what is right. On balance, we see this greater whole as a truer reflection of who we are, as compared to the instance of poor behavior. Do we see others in this same way?

Do we see the overall worth and the potential in others as greater than the mistakes they make—or do we see their mistakes as all of who they are? All of us are "works-in-progress," important and valuable despite the mistakes we make. As a leader it is your job to bring out the best in your staff. To bring out the best in others we need be looking for it.

When we regard others in this constructive way, they have a tendency for the most part to live up to our view of them. Your positive vision of others encourages and frees them, to seek and find their best ideals.

Nels: "Earlier in my career, my focus for success was on my individual effort and the ability to be better at a task than the other person. It was a very narrow approach that by its nature separated me from others, even if I was working on a task with them. My approach was centered on how my participation would help *me* to get ahead. This approach was supported by an organizational structure that had at its center the 'chain of command.' The objective for success was to move up the chain via individual effort. I tried to become an 'expert' in human resources and show leadership qualities, so that I could climb the supervisory ladder. It was all about me attaining my goals.

"When GTE/Sylvania got into 'Total Quality' the TQ concepts challenged my self-focused way of seeing things. Fortunately for me, I have always tried to maintain an objective sense about what I believed. I try to stay open to options that work better—produce better results. At first TQ was just something that Sylvania's general manager wanted me to learn about. The more I experienced it, however, the more I began to believe *that a greater base of ideas, knowledge, and methods, combined with a greater degree of cooperation and shared motivation, would result in a better outcome.*

"The key was to put systems in place that would allow this to occur (efficient use of data, effective meeting processes, rules for good teamwork, etc.). What I hadn't expected were the changes within me and in my relationships. The more you value the contributions of others, the more positively you view them in your mind's eye. Heightened respect for others in turn alters how they respond to you. Over time, you and your relationships are changed."

Life: In contemplating our lives, even when immersed in what seems to be the intransigent monolith of public education, are we seeing the opportunities and choices that we have? Do we regard ourselves as stuck in place, victims of the status quo, or do we recognize that our future, for the most part, is a reflection of our choices? Even in difficult circumstances, we can be molders and shapers of our future.

4. *The Hardest Thing About Problem Solving.* **Joe:** "The hardest aspect of problem solving is not necessarily identifying a solution, but is often: (a) beginning the process with people *standing together* with shared motivation to solve the problem, and (b) getting the problem *out on the table without triggering fearful emotions* or other forms of fight or flight.

"If we point fingers and become mired in blaming each other, then we are not in a position to reach a solution. If we fail to listen first, we will not have all the facts necessary to formulate a good solution. If we make 'you statements' and trigger emotions, we will have layered a more difficult and contentious problem on top of the problem we are already trying to solve. *The personal always trumps the problem.*

"If we are going to be excellent problem solvers, we must keep personal comments, accusations, and negative tones out of the process, focusing instead on the issue itself in an objective way. The outcome will always benefit if we keep in mind the importance of being respectful and objective, and operating within the parameters of the working values.

"For the last fifteen years I have been teaching a five-week parenting course for the Ipswich schools. As part of this course, a parent once shared an anecdote that underscored the importance of 'listening first' in a most compelling way. In the previous week's class I had talked with the parents about listening first and listening reflectively. Their homework had been to try reflective listening during the week if the opportunity presented itself. At the start of the next session, in the 'homework report' segment, the parent in question told the following story.

"An argument was brewing with her middle-school daughter about wearing dirty jeans to school. The parent wanted the daughter to wear something clean and the daughter insisted on wearing her dirty jeans. A power struggle was under way in earnest, when the mother very fortunately recalled the homework assignment. By stopping the power struggle, backing up, and practicing reflective listening, she gained her daughter's confidence, to the point where the daughter revealed the real problem. The daughter believed she was too heavy and felt that the only clothing she had that didn't make her look too heavy were the jeans in question.

"Needless to say, this revelation changed the discussion completely. By listening empathetically, the mother found that the problem wasn't about wearing clean clothes to school, but about her daughter's self-image. Now she could address the real issue.

"Being calm, respectful, cautious, thoughtful, and objective about how we initiate a discussion can enable us to get problems out on the table without triggering fear or other counterproductive emotions. Keys to successfully doing so are being sure we are mentally standing together looking at the problem from the same perspective—listening first, and then speaking with the pronoun 'I' (rather than the accusatory 'you'); and explaining how we feel while staying focused on the solution."

Figure 5.1 illustrates what we call the "problem solving position"—how the proper positioning of parties to a problem affords the greatest opportunity for a successful resolution.

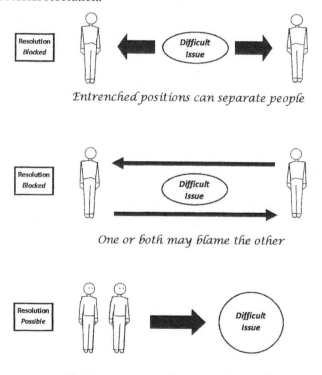

Entrenched positions can separate people

One or both may blame the other

Two or more standing together, willing and sufficiently open to approach the problem collaboratively, even thought they may start with differing views

Figure 5.1.   Problem-Solving Positions

We have included additional resources related to problem solving in appendix H.

5. *Good Criteria Make For Good Decisions.* When we are in a group of coworkers who have the responsibility for making a decision, it is important to consider the many different criteria that may exist in their minds as a basis

for making that decision. It would be a mistake to assume that everyone is mentally "on the same page." We may presume similarity, but that presumption is probably far from reality. People are likely to approach and regard problems from very different perspectives based on their life experiences. They may also evaluate results by different standards. This difference in people's thinking leads to scattered discussions and confused outcomes.

Ken: "In one of my first administrative positions I remember leading the faculty in a goal-setting process that quickly took a 'wrong turn.' My inexperience and naiveté were certainly contributing factors.

"I hadn't *prepped* the staff as to what we were going to be doing at the meeting. There were no prior discussions regarding criteria to guide the brainstorming and decision making. Nor was I engaging in the exercise because of a specific issue or incident that had occurred. I was just proceeding with the thought that there were plenty of areas where we could probably be doing a better job, so let's just talk about them and get some good things going. (Let's just go ahead and get something good done right away!) It seemed logical to me. It turned out to be another case of good intentions gone awry.

"Here are the top three areas for school improvement that the faculty offered that day: (1) fewer student supervisory duties for teachers (recess and before school), (2) fewer required parent conferences, and (3) fewer and shorter faculty meetings. Interspersed in the brainstorming were also a number of suggestions as to how I as principal could be doing a better job.

"While I dutifully recorded all that was brainstormed, and while some of what was offered was helpful for me to know, what didn't emerge were items that had to do with our working together on behalf of students. It was all self-focused. During this process I remember feeling my face 'heat up' as I experienced the unpleasant flush of embarrassment and frustration. I was very grateful when that meeting ended. I don't believe we ever revisited the 'goal list' from that day.

"By comparison, during the first year of utilizing the collaborative improvement process, the Doyon School staff successfully chose to focus on redefining our professional relationships. In the second year, the goal setting process began with the benefit of guidelines and activities provided by Joe and Nels. Prominent among the guidelines (which I placed at the top of the first faculty handout), were two sets of bullets addressing *criteria* for decision making. These were presented before the discussion as a starting point and they read as follows.

Our purpose is to create a School Improvement Plan that accomplishes the following key criteria:

- Produces the most benefit for students.
- Helps us to be focused and motivated in working together.

• Is the best use of our time.

To achieve that purpose we hope to create the following:

• A vision that is clear and motivating.
• A set of targeted goals that are focused, achievable, and worthy of a year's worth of our energies.
• A team structure that represents the best use of our knowledge, abilities, and interests.

After discussion, the teachers decided that the top three bullets were good criteria for making our decisions about mission, vision, goals, and objectives. The outcome of goal-setting work at the Doyon School was amazingly different from that which occurred in my prior school, because we had taken the time to discuss goal-setting criteria and because the criteria we chose called on us to 'put the needs of students first.'

"Deciding on the criteria for making a decision is a key part of the process. By uniting first on decision-making criteria, we become more likely to reach a meaningful and positive consensus."

6. *Understanding Mission and Vision.* Many organizations are conflicted by personalities who see life through very different filters. A mission or vision works for a family, a school, or a corporation by uniting us behind mutual aspirations and encouraging us to put aside differences. A strong mission or vision allows us to respond to new events from a proactive focused perspective, rather than operating from a reactive posture based on individual inclinations.

The mission or vision may be written or not—though written is much better. *What is most important is for it to be carried in the heart of the organization.* In a home it may be a desire to make our family a "sanctuary of support for each other." In a school it may be a desire to "better educate students so as to give them greater opportunities in life." In a corporation it may be a desire "to produce an outstanding product or service for our customers that makes us proud of what we are doing together." Whatever it is, the concepts and the words used to describe them must be truly valued by those who will be called upon to make it happen.

The mission and vision tell us who we want to be and where we want to go together, in a broad sense. Through the choice of *goals and objectives*, we become specific about how we want to achieve the mission and vision. The structure of the elements of the improvement process builds downward: Goals are chosen to attain the vision; objectives are chosen to achieve the goals; and action plans are chosen to bring each objective to life. All of these components combine to achieve the mission—through them we become who we've aspired to be.

Below is a list of definitions we developed to describe the elements of a focused improvement process—and to take some of the confusion out of conflicting terminology. Those working on the improvement process need to use the terms consistently. It is a good idea to correct inconsistent use of language until everyone becomes accustomed to the terminology.

Elements of the Improvement Process

If we are to excel we need to know who we want to be and where we want to go together:

> *Working Values*: Values that elevate working relationships (ongoing and amended as needed).

> *Mission*: A statement of who we are and who we hope to become (5–10 years).

> *Vision*: A statement of what we want to accomplish (3–5 years).

> *Goals*: Major steps to help the vision become a reality (1–3 years).

> *Objectives*: Prioritized steps that help each goal become a reality (until completed, one year at a time).

> *Action Plans*: Plans to achieve each objective, including persons responsible and a timeline (until completed, one year at a time).

7. What Do the Elements of the Improvement Process Do for Us? While they are meant to engage and unify, the mission, vision, and their attendant subparts assist us in other ways as well:

- They help us to prioritize the use of resources.
- They replace a reliance on central authority with a mutually held vision.
- They protect us from those who would impose their vision on us.
- They encourage alignment, enabling us to "pull the wagon" in the same direction.
- They generate a sense of empowerment, engaging individuals and moving them to proclaim, "I believe in the direction we are going and I will do my part to help us get there."

To bring mission and vision into reality we need to give light and air to the visionary inside each of us. We become united and inspired as we discover and articulate goal areas held in common. We become motivated as we gently compare where we are now to where we hope to go. As eloquently expressed by Peter Senge and Colleen Lannon-Kim in their essay, "Recapturing the Spirit of Learning through a Systems Approach" (AASA, 1994), the leader's job is to harness the creative tension between the *vision* and the *current reality*. (Senge also wrote with insight about creating "learning organizations" in his excellent book, *The Fifth Discipline*.)

PHASE III: STEPS TO PUT THE ELEMENTS OF THE IMPROVEMENT PROCESS IN PLACE

We'll address the steps of Phase III as a list, followed by an expanded discussion of each step.

Phase III Steps:

1. Formulate *vision and mission.*
2. Select *goals* to bring vision and mission to life.
3. Form *teams* to create objectives and action plans.
4. Choose *objectives* to bring the goals to life.
5. Draft *action plans* to accomplish each objective.

Phase III, Step 1: Formulate vision and mission. The Doyon School had an existing mission statement that the staff still saw as valid, so it was retained. It read as follows:

"As the Paul F. Doyon Memorial School learning community we believe in:

- *Citizenship*, with the goal of becoming a valued, contributing member of our school family and our community as a whole,
- *Responsibility*, with the goal of becoming a lifelong learner, and
- *Learning*, with a goal of recognizing and then implementing the skills needed for today, and building on what is needed for tomorrow."

It is very appropriate to build on the best of the past and not engage in a new process as if you were starting from a clean slate. Look for and honor work already done. Even if the organization is in need of improvement, people are always doing valuable work. This work should be recognized for its effort, and the best of it should be kept and built upon. We do not want to create alienation by unnecessarily denigrating previous work that members of the group may value. That is the opposite of the message we are trying to send about honoring the investment of time on behalf of students. Be sensitive to this issue as you introduce the process—it is important as a part of first impressions.

You can see from the above Doyon mission statement that the concepts are very global and did not reflect a clearly focused agenda. The school did not have a focused vision statement that stated succinctly where they wanted to go. Through a process we will describe, the school arrived at the vision statement, *"Literacy for All, Excitement for Learning."*

This is an outstanding example of a short, descriptive, motivating vision statement that tells what the school envisions for its future. It states that the Doyon School wants every student reading, writing, and performing math successfully, and that it wants all students to be personally committed to, and enthusiastically engaged in, their own education. These are keystones upon which a process of improvement can be built.

In setting mission, vision, and goals we first want to discover what each person believes about how to improve our school; then we proceed to discover which of those beliefs we hold in common.

This step involves the participation of the widest group of stakeholders because we want everyone on board with the broad scope of the school's direction. When we get down to goals and objectives, decision making becomes primarily the job of the professionals whose responsibility it will be to implement the goals (with continued coordination and support from the school council and input from parents).

At the higher mission and vision levels, we need the participation of a representative group of parents, the full faculty, school staff, administrators, and the school council if you have one, as well as representation from your central office. At the middle and high school levels, students should be participants. At the elementary school level we did not involve students, as this larger perspective of their education would be beyond their experience and knowledge, though we did take into account student opinion surveys and test results.

Survey outcomes are a valuable resource to consider, especially when setting goals and objectives. They could be useful in this step as well, as background information prior to discussion. It is your choice.

We haven't specifically included a survey in the steps to this point because formulation of vision and mission are about articulating dreams and hopes from a broad perspective. We want everyone to think broadly and deeply at the start. At this point, a survey might tend to make the discussion too issue specific and turn the focus toward a narrower problem-solving context. Again, you get to decide. For your use in composing surveys whenever you decide to use them, we have included a list of sample questions in appendix I. These surveys address administration, operations, culture, and attitudes, while leaving academic assessment to established standardized testing.

Vision, mission, and goals should not be a "fingers in the dike" exercise in fixing problems—or "putting out fires"—but instead should be about purposefully creating far-reaching positive structures that will naturally displace problems.

We suggest breaking down formulating vision and mission into four sub-steps.

A. First, reach agreement *on the criteria* to be used in choosing mission, vision, goals, and objectives. We suggest something similar to the bulleted criteria list that Ken used at the Doyon School (see the "Good Criteria" section #5 earlier in this chapter) as a starting point for the discussion. We suggest that the group strive collectively to identify that which (1) will produce the most benefit for students, (2) will encourage us to be focused and motivated in working together as a staff, and (3) is the best use of our time.

It might be enough just to agree on one overriding criterion: *What is best for students*. In any case, hold a discussion and come to consensus on your decision-making criteria. Criteria can be weighted, such as giving the benefit of students a weight of two and other criteria a weight of one. If meeting the needs of students isn't the top priority, you will *not* have a vision, mission, and set of goals capable of pulling you together and calling you to higher levels of collaborative accomplishment—at least that is our experience.

B. Next, pose or review prior responses to the following *two questions*:

1. If things went great in our school over the next five years, what positive changes do you project occurring that would be of the most benefit to students?
2. What caused these positive changes to happen?

You should have already completed this "If Things Went Great" exercise as a part of Phase I. That exercise is built around answering the first question above. Distribute the results of that exercise prior to or at the meeting to refresh memories. Begin the meeting by reviewing the results. If you haven't completed the "Causes of Positive Change" exercise (question 2 above), refer to the directions in appendix F, and conduct that brainstorming exercise now.

Invite the group to envision the improvements of that future school in their mind's eye. Let them be present there. Let them jot down a few notes and think about it. Then go around the group asking for responses to the second question, *"What caused the positive change you envisioned to happen?"* The facilitator can ask people as they speak to go a bit deeper and explain their thinking. Contemplating possible causes produces real food for thought and it will certainly change the possible options and solutions that you discuss.

Do not allow crosstalk the first time around, except to ask for clarification. Let people get their thoughts out clearly without interruption. With a smaller group, keep everyone together; have one discussion. Use something like our "Roundtable" format described in appendix G. Display the results.

Have a second round and allow some crosstalk at that time. With a larger group, you can brainstorm using the TEAM format also found in appendix G.

The development of consensus regarding decision-making criteria and responses to the two questions above should be repeated with your parent organization, nonfaculty staff, and the school council. Make them generally aware of the principal and faculty input. We want them to be aware of what's important to the principal and faculty, but to also be creative and fresh in adding their own ideas into the mix.

C. The third substep is to *recruit a drafting committee of four to six persons to review the criteria and the responses to the two questions from all groups.* Contained in the answers to the two questions will be the outcomes and causes that your stakeholders see as most important to the future of the school. From these answers it will be possible to select options to start the discussion of mission, vision, and goals.

The drafting committee should organize the input from the different groups into a coherent form prior to beginning their deliberations. One approach would be to collect and post all the input of the different groups on chart paper and then underline or highlight important ideas and catchy phrases. Drawing primarily from what is highlighted, *the drafting committee then develops options for mission, vision, and major goals.*

D. The fourth substep is for the drafting committee to *bring the options developed above to a joint conference of representatives of the different groups. The conference will decide on a mission, vision, and possibly broad goals or themes.* Be certain that the principal and faculty endorse the conference results. If they have concerns, bring these issues back to a second meeting of the conference until they are resolved.

The *mission* is a statement of who we are and who we hope to become. So extract from the input the most fundamental beliefs about who "you" are and the kind of organization you want to have. Pare it down. Keep it brief. A few *sentences* at the most should do it. If the mission statement is longer, it will get filed away and forgotten no matter how well written it is. People will say, "Oh yeah, don't we have that in the mission statement? Let's look in the files and see what it says." If we have to look it up in the files, it is not alive. (Think of the files as a drawer in a morgue.) Keep the mission statement relatively brief; make it memorable.

The *vision* statement should be one or two *phrases*, a short sentence maybe. It should sum up where you want to go together. It should be catchy and motivating. For example, when working on creating an early childhood education center, a leadership committee for that project selected the following vision statement: *"All families ready for school. All schools ready for families."* This statement does an excellent job of envisioning a school–home collaborative partnership that will benefit children. Spending hours and hours getting together lots of beautiful verbiage is not productive; all that is needed is clear, brief, motivating language.

Involving the group in the process of choosing a mission and vision builds ownership. Keep in mind that the power of mission and vision statements is not in the verbiage—regardless of how articulate—but is rather in whether they elicit motivation and buy-in.

Phase III, Step 2: Select goals to bring vision and mission to life. The clarity of the two-part Doyon vision statement, *"Literacy for All, Excitement for Learning,"* lent itself to creating two initial goals:

- Improving the reading program, and
- Organizing a series of special events to build excitement for learning.

In selecting goals, there is no easy formula. We are constantly looking to balance alignment and empowerment, continuity and innovation, relationships and rigor. We start with a list of potential goals that emerge from the responses to the two basic questions from Step 1, substep B. Then focus on the vision and mission statements we have framed, recognizing that the purpose of the goals is to bring these statements to life.

Before addressing the mechanics of goal selection, let us interject a reminder about *objectivity.* We broached this subject in chapter 3. *At the outset of goal selection it is vital to discuss with everyone the concept of staying objective until the best goals reveal themselves.*

Assuming hardened positions early in the dialogue will short-circuit the possibility of reaching the best and most creative solutions. Before the best ideas have a chance to surface, people may start boxing themselves in by early positioning that begins turning on defense mechanisms in others.

Ask that the group begin by looking over the goal list provided by the drafting committee. Encourage and discuss suggestions for adding, deleting, or amending items. Create a full list of possible goals. When your list of goal options is complete, perform a "quick prioritization" right away (refer to appendix F). A prioritized list of goal options may also be created using the TEAM exercise (see appendix G).

All ideas are not created equal. There is a need to find out right away which goals are the highest priorities for the group as a whole.

You will save a great deal of valuable time by not discussing the pros and cons of all the ideas as if they were equal. Only take the time to discuss fully those that have substantial group support. After the prioritization exercise, potential goals will have arranged themselves in an order reflective of the group's interest. Together pick a cut-off point allowing the goals above the cut-off score into the pro and con discussion. Assure everyone that no ideas will be lost. The full list is kept for the next time the school chooses a new goal in the ongoing process—all previously listed goals come alive again at that point. This method signals respect for everyone's ideas, but acknowledges that certain goals have a priority with the group at this time.

Then bring out your key criteria again and ask the following questions: Which of the remaining goals would

- do the most for students?
- do the most to make our mission and vision come alive?
- be the most motivating for us?
- be the wisest use of our time?
- be achievable and within our control?

Weigh each option against the criteria, discussing pros and cons. Remember that an objective charting of pros and cons will help you to end up unified and focused behind a couple of goals. It is especially important that administrators resist any temptation to lobby hard for a "favorite" list of outcomes or a particular goal as opposed to objectively facilitating the process. That would be a violation of trust.

While it's certainly OK (and desirable) for the principal to participate in the discussions, the principal's main role should be one of "process protector." If the group gets off track and stalls or becomes adversarial, pull them back to a point of unity and start to move forward again—respectfully and together. Do not let violations of the working values slip in and scuttle the process.

It would be ideal if at the end of this discussion two top prioritized goals were chosen—one academic and one focusing on school climate or culture (which includes student motivation)—thus leading to the creation of two teams. This makes for a very workable process.

In selecting goals, consider the use of a Venn diagram. A Venn diagram, for instance, could show us the intersection of what is best for kids and what we are most motivated to accomplish. We draw two large overlapping circles: In one put the top priorities on our list of prospective changes that will most benefit students; in the other list the items we as a group are most motivated to accomplish. In the space where the circles overlap, place the items that are in both circles. These items can be a great place from which to select our next goal.

Before we began the process, we selected a book of charts and tools to be used to aid various aspects of the process. We found *Power-Up Teams and Tools*, by Dr. William Montgomery, to be an excellent source of tools such as affinity diagrams, flow charts, cause and effect diagrams, decision matrixes, and radar charts. It came in handy on numerous occasions, and we recommend that you acquire such a compilation as well.

Phase III, Step 3: Form teams to create objectives and action plans. The Doyon vision lent itself to the formation of two teams: (1) the Literacy Team, and (2) the Excitement for Learning Team. In later years when we had three teams, we found that they started to "bump into" each other and cause jurisdiction issues. We also found that adding too many teams started to divide (and hence weaken) our focus, so we recommend two teams as best, one working with *academic/curriculum goals* and the other focused on *school culture/climate goals.* You can name your teams according to the area of school life they represent such as the academic team and the school culture team.

The mission of the academic team is contained in its name—all things academic, principally those having to do with curriculum and instruction. The school culture team's mission is less obvious. This team focuses on issues that include love of learning, discipline protocols, bullying, character development, social and emotional learning, peer relations, student leadership, and student motivation.

The two teams can have subgroups to address different objectives, such as one subgroup researching a longer-term project while another is working on a shorter-term project. This speaks to having teams of 12–15 members, or enough so that the team can have two decent sized subgroups when necessary.

While attendance and participation at scheduled faculty meetings is of course not optional, assuming leadership roles or drafting/research responsibilities, etc. are strictly voluntary. You may want to recruit certain teachers to lead or facilitate (or colead) groups because of their background or areas of expertise, but in general let faculty members join the team they choose. The exception would be if you needed more of a mix of grade level, subject, or specialist representation. If that is the case, you may have to ask a few persons if they would be willing to switch teams. Teams can be unequal in size.

Each team regularly reports progress back to the faculty, and full faculty meetings are used for the times when pivotal evaluations or decisions have to be made. This is an efficient method, but again, if the teams don't pay particular attention to keeping the entire faculty informed and involved, then when a presentation is made, the ideas will come at the faculty as too new, perhaps unexpected, and could prompt anxiety, resulting in discord.

Frequent communication is essential. Give reports of progress. Pay strict attention to bringing everyone along with ideas as they unfold, consistently seeking discussions with, and input from, persons beyond the team. Invite non–team members to important workshops or on observational visits to see programs of particular interest firsthand.

Don't "spring" any surprises on the larger group; it will create discord. Discord is like Humpty Dumpty falling—better to avoid than to try to set right afterward.

Develop a very clear charge for each team and put it in writing. You may use the minutes of faculty meetings to record team assignments, such as this team charge: "The Academic Team will pursue planning that will help the school select and implement a new reading program. The research, options, and recommendations of the team will be brought back to the full faculty for periodic discussion and final approval. The team will make interim reports of progress to the faculty and principal so that there are no surprises. The first report of progress will be in December, with a final report of options for choosing a reading program due in March."

Provide teams with training right away to enhance effectiveness. It helps to have team leaders who have already received training as a result of serving on the coordinating team.

We have provided *team training resources* to be certain that "consensus" is understood and to increase the likelihood that team meetings and the process steps will be productive:

- "A Guide to Effective Meetings" is provided in appendix A.
- "A Guide to Consensus" can be found in appendix B.
- Diagrams outlining the steps for both planning and problem solving are presented in appendix H.

Phase III, Step 4: Choose objectives to bring the goals to life. Framing objectives prioritizes the steps toward accomplishing the goals. Each goal has its own set of objectives. As with *vision* and *goals*, deciding on *objectives* requires making choices. Each level of choosing sharpens the focus of your improvement initiative.

When you choose an objective, it means not choosing several others. You are selecting, in order of implementation, the two or three initial steps that will most help the goal to come to life. Let's say your culture team goal is to "reduce the amount of bullying in the school." A reasonable set of objectives might include (1) administering a survey to determine the extent and type of bullying that is happening in the school; (2) providing training for school personnel in recognizing bullying and learning techniques of intervention to stop demeaning behavior; and (3) engaging the student body in an initiative to increase supportive, empathetic behavior.

The survey would come first because we have to know the nature of the behavior we are going to target. For example, student surveys in Ipswich showed that the word "bullying," as defined by Ipswich students, for the most part referred not to physical threat, but to mental and emotional harassment. The bullying behavior consisted mostly of mean talk, teasing, demeaning comments, exclusionary behavior, and repeated verbal put-downs. If we made assumptions without data, we might be focusing, at least in part, on the wrong problem.

When we prioritize objectives and put them in a logical sequential order, we establish a step-by-step approach toward achievement of the goal. It gives us a plan to follow.

In the antibullying goal example, a top objective might well have been to bring in antibullying speakers and programs. However, survey results clearly indicated that students were already uniformly against bullying conceptually; the problem was that they weren't taking action based on their beliefs. They did not need additional antibullying rhetoric. What they needed were specific actions to build a more empathetic peer culture and to encourage students to be more proactive against bullying when it occurred.

We need to understand the problem in order to choose objectives that make a difference.

Objectives and the *action plans* based on them do not have to be perfect. All they have to do is to improve our position from where we are now.

Never let the desire to be "perfect" stop you from improving. All we need do is take a step forward. When we take enough steps forward, we will have made the outstanding progress that we were seeking. Objectives are steps forward.

Phase III, Step 5: Draft action plans to accomplish each objective. Each objective calls for an action plan. The action plan contains the following information.

- What will be done?
- Who will do it?
- Who will be responsible for supervising progress towards the plan?
- How will we measure progress?
- What is the timeline for reports of progress and completing the plan?
- What resources will we need?
- Who will be in support of the responsible persons?
- Will there be milestones that we can celebrate?

Note that "supervision" as used above means supervision of the process steps, seeing that the process steps move along; it does not mean making decisions for the group—the important decisions in collaborative improvement planning are made by group consensus.

After the planning stage, whether the same persons will be a part of *participating in implementation* is up to the principal. Once a plan is approved and becomes operational, the principal is in operational control. The principal can allow the teams or team members an oversight role if she or he chooses. It is natural for teams or the full faculty to want to follow up on plans they created. This can work well, just as long as their oversight stops short of any teacher giving orders to other teachers or staff members.

The action plan should be written in a format that clarifies responsibilities. The principal and the faculty collaborate in creating action plans. It is then the principal's task to see that the specific objectives and their action plans are recorded in a file, that timetables are met, and that the action plan is ultimately accomplished.

Keep in mind that action plans often call for *training* that is a key to successful implementation. Good training prepares people to succeed. We strongly recommend prioritizing use of professional development funds to support your school's goals. Over recent years, there have been limited funds for professional development in the Ipswich schools. We believe that when these limited resources are available, they should be used mostly in direct support of our goals.

We have found that the best results and the biggest "bang for the buck" come from offering local onsite training (the quality and content of which you can control)—training that targets some aspect of your improvement plan. This allows more people to be trained and has the biggest impact on your improvement initiatives.

Ken: "While implementing action plans never let the 'tail wag the dog.' At Doyon, in order to implement our improvement plans, there were occasions when almost everyone in the school was inconvenienced in order to get clear blocks of instructional time for primary reading and math. The benefit to students was enormous. If everybody hadn't been involved in formulating the plans, if everyone wasn't putting students first, the level of 'good-faith' cooperation that took place in these schedule changes could never have happened.

"The school came to believe that the schedule should be in support of maximizing student learning and that all other considerations and conveniences ought to be secondary to that purpose."

If we are truly "putting students first," we ought not to let changes beneficial to students be put aside because they might inconvenience adults. We do want to be reasonable, however, and it is possible to ask too much or implement too fast. If this is a concern, we can moderate pace, phase changes in, try limited piloting, and consider other reasonable ways to address concerns; but we should never cast aside an excellent change that we know will benefit students. Instead, search for a reasonable and sustainable way to get it done.

A REVIEW OF CHAPTER 5 CONCEPTS

- Accomplishment is the glue that binds a successful organization.
- A school's staff will put aside egos in favor of a vision and goals they believe in.

- Maximizing the positive in our attitude toward self, others, and life requires being aware of the choices being made in our inner conversations.
- Our improvement priorities for the year are focused when we can display them in a one-page improvement plan.
- We can lessen defensive reactions by listening first, and then, when it is our turn, speaking in terms of "I" rather than "you."
- Follow the Phase III steps to create an improvement process with these elements: mission, vision, goals, teams, objectives, and action plans.
- Decision-making criteria help us unite behind beneficial, student-oriented goals.
- Focusing our goals by limiting their number at any one time is not an option but a necessity to building motivation and momentum.
- We recommend forming two ongoing teams: one for academics and the second for school culture. Each team should work on only one or at the maximum two goals at a time.
- Objectives are prioritized steps toward attainment of a goal.
- Action plans describe what will be done, who will do it, who is supervising, the timeline, resources needed, and how progress will be measured in achieving the objectives.

Chapter Six

Building Cycles of Success

In this chapter we answer the question, "What does it take to go from an initial achievement to an ongoing succession of achievements?"

THE FUEL THAT MAKES THE TWIN ENGINES RUN

The twin engines of our process are

1. outstanding working relationships, and
2. collaborative, focused planning for improvement. To keep those engines running, we need to add another ingredient:
3. the *fuel* that runs the twin engines is *a commitment to continuous improvement*.

Our formula for creating a self-renewing system now looks like figure 6.1.

Outstanding Working Relationships
PLUS
Collaborative, Focused Improvement Planning
PLUS
A Commitment to Continuous Improvement
EQUALS
Cycles of Success

Figure 6.1. Self-Renewing System

THE TRANSITION FROM ONE SUCCESS
TO MULTIPLE SUCCESSES

Ken: "First, we want our staff to experience the satisfaction of an initial success (which we have so carefully nurtured!); next, we want them to believe that this same type of collaborative success can be repeated.

"Our initial two-year improvement plan at the Doyon School was very successful, but as it neared its end, I became apprehensive regarding what to do next.

"I was concerned that our collaborative effort might become a one-time 'flash in the pan.' Would we drift back into business as usual? I really wanted the enthusiasm, motivation, and collegiality to continue. It was so much better than any working environment I'd ever experienced. I sensed that the group also was feeling good about their collaborative accomplishments and that the energy was still flowing. I consulted with Joe and Nels for guidance regarding the next phase. I remember asking specifically whether vision, mission, and goals had a 'shelf life.' The advice they gave me included the following important principle:

"Only change a broad direction if it has outlived its usefulness or no longer reflects your priorities. Once an individual goal or objective becomes embedded into the regular operation of the school, replace it in the planning process with your next priority.

"This guideline helped me to formulate the substance of the faculty meetings that spring. I explained to my staff that now it was time to reflect upon what we had accomplished, assess it, and edit, change, and revitalize our goals as needed. It was time to draft a new plan that accurately reflected our priorities for the next improvement cycle.

"We held our first Roundtable session, and it was encouraging to hear that the faculty felt very positive about what we had accomplished. No one said anything to disparage the worth of the process. On the contrary, the consensus was that we had worked together effectively and had made substantial progress toward our goals.

"After listening to a full discussion of where we were and where we wanted to go, I used the weeks between meetings to draft an outline of a new improvement plan. I met with the school council and the parent organization to share our faculty discussions and the draft proposals for the new plan. I then presented the revised outline to the full faculty and explained that I needed to know from them if I was 'on the right track.'

"I did not ask them to *approve* my proposal. I did not want to get into the rubber-stamping dynamic again. I intended my outline as just a reflection of our ongoing conversation. The initial feedback was so positive, however, that about two-thirds of the way into that meeting I felt comfortable asking for a thumbs up/thumbs down *informal* 'dipstick vote.' That was how we reached consensus on our next two-year plan. Every two years for the ensuing decade, we revised our goals and objectives.

"Here are some thoughts that emerged from that ongoing goal-setting process.

1. *Coordination:* Someone has to own responsibility for collecting the faculty input that emerges from brainstorming, Roundtable meetings, or informal discussions. The material needs condensing so that themes can emerge and areas of potential consensus can surface. I decided that this was an important role for the principal and that I was comfortable taking it on. It can also be done in consultation with or as delegated to a small team suited to that purpose.

2. *Who is the Hub in Setting the Goals:* The answer for the most part should be the *faculty*. I told the teachers at the outset that unless I felt we were about to act in a way that was bad for kids or that violated our core values, I would not replace their goal-setting priorities or judgments with my own.

While I made an effort to keep everyone 'in the loop' as we drafted new plans, and while I shared my thoughts freely and sought input from other groups (e.g., nonfaculty staff, the parent organization, and the school council), I made it clear to all that faculty consensus support was the single most *essential* ingredient for a successful school improvement initiative. This, along with my stated willingness to go back and revise any part of what we had done, set the tone for our continued collaboration.

3. *Who Writes the Plan:* I asked the school council to write the final draft of each year's improvement plan, and to base their work on everyone's input. If you have no school council, appoint a committee charged with that purpose.

4. *The 'Slow-It-Downers' and the 'Speed-It-Uppers':* You can anticipate that in faculty discussions, there will be those who will express caution regarding the introduction of new goals—these are the 'slow-it-downers.' They will request additional time to focus on implementation of current goals. On the opposite end of the spectrum are those who may already be branching out to address additional areas and who are recommending that we incorporate new goal areas in the next improvement cycle—they are the 'speed-it-uppers.' Teachers in this group are naturally inclined to want to keep moving forward at a relatively fast pace.

"These two groups are not 'fringe elements'—they are important and substantial segments of the full spectrum of the faculty. You will need to acknowledge and accommodate both positions. There were years when everyone would be collectively focusing on full implementation of programs related to the existing set of goals, while a volunteer subteam of 'speed-it-uppers' concurrently explored an emerging goal area. In this way, the subgroup was able to help the full staff jump-start progress toward new goals at the start of the following year. The objective was to utilize the energy available for moving forward, while not 'losing' any substantial component of the staff to a feeling of being overwhelmed.

5. *Provide the Time:* Set aside time for teams to work on improvement goals. We replaced half of our full faculty meetings with 'team' meetings— either grade-level teams if program implementation was the priority or multi-grade 'vertical' subject-area teams if curriculum development/coordination was the focus. At times we hired substitutes for coverage so improvement work didn't always occur before or after the regular day.

6. *Review the History and the Fundamentals:* As we began each new school improvement plan, I met with the faculty to look back over what we had accomplished while also reviewing the fundamental beliefs and principles that underlie this type of shared leadership process. Sometimes this was a brief and informal few minutes at the start of an opening faculty meeting. In other years, particularly when there had been staff turnover, I spent more time planning and presenting this type of overview. I wanted to be sure that everyone knew why we had intentionally put this process into place and where we were in the flow and evolution of the goal/implementation cycle.

"People need to digest where they have been, and understand the 'why' of where they are before they can meaningfully participate in the selection of the best way to move forward.

"In addition to coordinating the improvement process, I encourage you as principal to assume the mantle of process historian, philosopher, and cheerleader."

PHASE IV: STEPS TO BUILD CYCLES OF SUCCESS

In this fourth phase we've identified ten steps to help you establish ongoing cycles of collaborative improvement.

Phase IV Steps:

1. Make a commitment to continuous improvement.
2. Sustain continuous improvement through mindful hiring.
3. Collect and value data.
4. Use proven planning and problem-solving processes.
5. Engage in systems thinking.
6. Get out of the bunker.
7. Let teachers be program builders.
8. Break deadlocks and overcome roadblocks.
9. Display and celebrate progress.
10. Review and renew goals and objectives.

"Phase IV, Step 1: Make a commitment to continuous improvement. Toward the end of each school year we recommend raising the question, *"How have we been doing?"* If it is also the end of a goal cycle, follow that with a discussion focusing on *"What is the next best thing for us to do?"* In other words, initiate a reflective self-assessment, which naturally leads to updating goals—tweaking or deleting some, keeping others, and adopting new goals.

Frame a *sequence of good questions.* Below are a few "discussion starters" Ken used during the first years of the Doyon School initiative—a period during which the improvement process could have fizzled out or continued with increasing power as it did.

When initially considering goals and objectives, Ken asked,

- How do we make the vision come alive?
- Is the goal worthy of our school working on it for a year?
- Is it good for students?
- Is it good for teachers?
- Is it good for parents?
- Are we in control of it?
- Is funding available?
- Is it measurable?
- Does it influence other goals in a positive way?

After these discussions, Ken and his staff brainstormed possible goals, worked with the other stakeholders, and finally framed prioritized goals and objectives.

The first major two-year review featured use of the "roundtable" meeting format (see appendix G) during which Ken posed these questions: *"Have we made progress? Where should we go from here?"* The opportunity to speak to each question went around the circle twice, with cross-comments allowed the second time. The notetaker recorded the ideas that emerged (without names) and distributed to all stakeholders for use at upcoming meetings.

At the end of the renewal dialogue, the following questions had been answered.

- Have we made progress on existing goals? *Yes.*
- Are the existing goals still worthwhile? *Yes.*
- Can any be dropped? *No.*
- Is the Vision still supported? *Yes.*
- Is the team format still supported? *Yes.*
- Are there emerging challenges and demands that we need to consider? *Yes.*
- Is there consensus regarding emerging priorities? *Yes.*

- Which of the following criteria should be the primary basis for focusing future efforts?

  - Most positive benefits to students?
  - Most positive results-to-effort ratio?
  - Most motivating for faculty and staff?
  - Most positive impact on test scores?
  - Most positive impact on parents and families?
  - Clarity of purpose—most clearly focused?

Ken and his team decided to incorporate as many of these motivators as they could into the planning, but the strongest emphasis remained on what was *best for students.*

In the sixth-year review, Ken was still asking questions to prompt a productive dialogue:

- How have we been doing?
- Have we made some progress?
- Is focused energy and effort still needed?
- Given our present areas of focus, where do we go from here?
- Should we add, edit, or drop any of our present goals or objectives?
- What are the next logical goals and objectives in our present areas of concentration?
- *If you had your own child in this school, what would you want him or her to know or be able to do beyond what we are presently teaching?*

  - What kind of learning experiences does it take to make these things happen?
  - How do we move toward the desired results?
  - Is there real value for us in this new area of interest?
  - Will this produce the most benefit for students?

A succession of well-framed questions, during a series of sessions dedicated to review and renewal, refocuses the process and keeps it moving forward.

Nels and Joe: "In our early work with the Ipswich schools, we spoke with each faculty, and conducted workshops throughout the system. At these workshops, continuous improvement was a key topic. We wanted everyone to know that they were embarking on an ongoing 'process,' not a one-time program.

"We explained that improvement efforts were cumulative, like climbing stairs or building with bricks. We cautioned against trying to get everything done at once; for achievement to be sustainable, we must take one step at a time. We advised each school to keep building layer upon layer, one row of bricks at a time, and that after a while they would notice they had built something substantial. It is important for people to visualize the task in that sustainable and cumulative way.

"We further explained that a commitment to continuous improvement was a belief in

- the creativity and wisdom of the group;
- our ongoing ability to plan and solve problems together;
- our capacity to stand together and meet any challenges that arise; and
- our ability to progress through repeated cycles of data, reflection, and action."

Phase IV, Step 2: Sustain continuous improvement through mindful hiring. In any work force, people leave and new people arrive. You can lose the continuous-improvement dynamic if new employees are not well informed about, and committed to, the school's process for improving. Who you hire is an important factor in your ongoing success.

Nels: "In my thirty years of human resources work I learned that there is nothing more important in hiring than ascertaining the critical skills necessary for the position and making sure your potential new hire has those skills. Have a well-thought-out job description for every position. Don't just list the duties; also include vital skills, including interpersonal skills you are looking for in the applicants. Interpersonal skills and the ability to participate in a collaborative environment are crucial considerations in hiring people who will be participating in this type of process. Ken and his staff developed an excellent team hiring process that he will describe."

Ken: "I approached the hiring of new teachers with both anxiety and excitement. There are few decisions that have as much of an impact on education as the choice of personnel—this is true for the students' educational experience, and also for us, the faculty and staff, in terms of school culture and teamwork. In addition to the usual considerations regarding credentials, experience, style, and other factors one would typically assess, we also considered whether we thought the applicant would participate in and contribute to our shared-leadership improvement model.

"The group dynamic becomes 'at risk' if new staff aren't well-informed about the school's model for improving. Some teachers prefer just to be shown what to teach and then to be allowed to close their classroom door (figuratively as well as literally)—they don't want to invest more than that. That might be fine in a school run in a top-down hierarchical manner (well, maybe not 'fine,' but at least not so counter to the school's intent), but for us it would be highly detrimental. So how do you know who you are hiring, really? The answer is, you don't, not with 100 percent certainty—but the following is what we did in order to maximize the likelihood of a 'good fit.'

We regularly hired *as a team*. We did so for three reasons:

1. I wanted to be sure that the new teacher would begin with the endorsement and support of colleagues—I didn't want this to be an 'arranged marriage' ('Hello grade two team—let me introduce the person I selected as your new team member'), but rather, a 'romance.'
2. I was once advised that if I hired alone, the trend would be toward a one-dimensional staff reflecting my personal predilections (e.g., my Meyers-Briggs type), as opposed to hiring with a team that would contribute to building a richer mix of abilities and styles.
3. I believe that a group, through discussions and the comparison of perceptions, can more accurately assess the qualifications of applicants than a single person can (i.e., in hiring, 'we' is better than 'me').

The hiring team, usually no more than five members including myself, was composed of grade-level or department colleagues, along with representation from our special needs faculty. Early in the process, prior to screening the applications, we would meet and set timelines and hiring ground rules (e.g., everyone attends all the interviews), and protocols (e.g., complete confidentiality). I also informed the hiring team that they each had a virtual '*stop*' button (and that I had one as well), so regardless of who the rest of the committee was recommending, if a member felt we should absolutely not hire an applicant, it was over. I always emphasized that this *power* should be used cautiously and judiciously—but providing it built trust.

Most importantly, in the pre-interview phase, we brainstormed *criteria for hiring*. We kept these criteria in mind as we sifted through the stacks of resumes to determine who to interview, developed interview questions, and actually conducted the interviews. Obviously each position carried its own profile reflective of the related educational responsibilities; but one criteria that was placed close to the top of the list was whether we sensed the applicant *was the type of person who would be willing to go beyond the ' given ' and lend their discretionary energies to improvement efforts.*

We tried to provide all interviewees a sense of who we were and of what their scope of responsibility would be if they joined us. If learning more about us appeared to energize them and make them even more determined to join us, great. If they appeared uncertain, uncomfortable, or wary, well, that added some uncertainty for us as well.

Immediately after each interview we would take a few minutes and go around the table sharing our perceptions and assigning each interviewee a score of 1–5, with 'five' being equivalent to recommending the applicant as a finalist and a 'one' signaling, 'no way.'

Ultimately, final hiring decisions sometimes come down to intuitive gut responses and only time tells whether the team has made the best decision.

All you can do is to try your best to minimize discrepancies between impression and reality. Usually you know whether you've judged correctly in the first year (or two at the most).

"To ensure that expectations were clear from the start, I made it a practice to orient each new teacher in a 1:1 session prior to the start of the year. In addition to reviewing all standard necessities associated with routines and teaching responsibilities, I also shared with them that it was my hope, and indeed my expectation, that over the course of their first years with us they would find a way to contribute that would make us a better school."

Phase IV, Step 3: Collect and value data. Knowing the truth of where you are is nothing but good. You can't get to where you hope to go without knowing where you are at the start. How do you find out? Collect data.

We can have accurate situational awareness through data, or be flying blind and making decisions based on subjective opinion, conjecture, the leader's gut sense, or passionate guessing.

There is a big difference between a leadership approach that relies on accurate facts and one that makes decisions based on anecdotal information. It doesn't matter if the data collected reveals unforeseen problems—in reality, that is helpful. It's never a bad thing to know where you are. Knowing what is really happening gives us the chance to make it better. So don't be afraid of collecting data.

We are where we are; we can either know it or not.

Determine what type of data to collect. We can measure facts or we can measure opinion—each has a valid use. Data can be direct or indirect, objective or subjective. Standardized national reading tests are considered direct and objective, as are SAT exams. A survey of parents, teachers, or students about school issues would be considered mostly subjective. Yet, such surveys are accessible and have great value. Those closest to students know the students best and have good insight into what students need; this information is especially useful when their insights are combined in a group survey.

Surveys are a meaningful way of examining strengths and weaknesses, and are especially valuable at the start of any thorough planning process.

Working with the school principals in Ipswich, Nels and Joe developed surveys for students, teachers, and parents. They are administered on a rotating basis, one group per year. Results are analyzed, and the data/trends influence planning and policy decisions at the schools. (We provide a set of sample survey questions in appendix I.)

To diminish anxieties, we use surveys as in-house working documents. Schools are public institutions, so we don't want data taken out of context and appearing in local headlines. Using your surveys as in-house working documents will encourage candor both in responses and in the analysis of the results.

When analyzing survey data, we have consistently found that some results are better than we expected, and other aspects revealed a concern we had not anticipated. There are always differences between reality and our perception of it. If decisions about programs for the future are made based on initial inaccurate information, those decisions will be flawed from the start.

Data may reveal negatives; but further collaborative reflection and interpretation can help us identify and build positives to displace those negatives.

Phase IV, Step 4: Use proven planning and problem-solving processes. A good improvement process begins with the notion that to improve something we must first understand it. How is it working now? How do people feel about it? What are the causes of problems? What aspects offer the most promise for growth?

We provide diagrams outlining our approach to planning and problem solving in appendix H. They will help you to remember important steps while avoiding possible missteps. As we've recommended in previous chapters, a team should agree to the process steps it will take at the start of its deliberations so everyone knows where they are going and how they are going to get there. When setting goals and objectives, and again when implementing those goals and objectives, agree upon the steps for moving forward. Use the planning and problem-solving processes as a guide to select the set of steps.

A school that wishes to choose a new reading or math series, for example, might agree to the following general steps: research programs, visit schools using programs of interest, consider the pros and cons of the various programs, select a program to pilot in several classrooms, and make the decisions if and when to go school-wide.

Both planning and problem solving benefit from carefully considering and designing each step prior to action; but they differ in purpose. If you are engaged in considering what goal or objective comes next, use a *planning process.* A planning process is distinguished from problem solving by being larger in scope and open concerning the direction of goals. Planning begins with an evaluation of strengths and weaknesses that helps us decide where to focus our efforts. This can be accomplished by a discussion similar to those in step 1 of this chapter. How are we doing? How do we feel about what has been accomplished so far? What is most important to do next?

Unlike a planning process, a *problem-solving process* begins with a narrower specific problem; it then goes on to help us find the best solution for that problem. Problem-solving steps involve (1) making sure that the identified problem really is the problem; (2) determining the causes of the problem; (3) using as a benchmark other schools that are handling the problem well; (4) creating optional solutions; (5) evaluating the pros and cons of each optional solution; (6) testing solutions; and (7) implementing a solution.

Ken: "We often 'tried out' solutions to problems by applying them in a few places or for a limited period before we incorporated them into regular practice; this 'pilot/tryout' approach worked well as applied to many aspects of school life including curriculum (e.g., several classes trying a new approach to spelling or handwriting), broad program changes (e.g., piloting a full-day kindergarten in one classroom), or something as 'simple' as rerouting movement through the halls for entry and dismissal routines.

"Piloting helped us avoid spinning our wheels and getting stuck looking for a 'perfect' analysis or solution. Instead, we would try something in a limited way, and then see how it went before broader adoption."

The planning and problem-solving charts in appendix H are based on standard models modified to include additional steps we see as requisite for an outstanding outcome.

Phase IV, Step 5: Engage in systems thinking. A quality management approach calls for analyzing operating systems with the purpose of eliminating unnecessary or redundant efforts and adding value wherever we can. We examine how we are functioning, and then we try to find simpler, smarter, and more effective ways of accomplishing the same tasks. Systems analysis helps us to discover means of increasing efficiency, productivity, and the quality of our product or service.

W. Edwards Deming, the quality management guru, wrote that most organizational problems were systemic in nature, and not the result of human error or incompetence. The following story from Ken powerfully illustrates this point.

Ken: "One of my first teaching jobs was as a science 'cluster' teacher (a New York City Board of Education term for an elementary teacher who teaches a single subject and moves from class to class) in the East Harlem area of Manhattan. Most of the students came from economically disadvantaged homes. Many were being raised by single parents. Drugs were everywhere. Used syringes littered the streets. At dismissal I would sometimes see students leave the school, cross the street, and take the hand of an older brother or sister, who had been nodding off in front of the local pizza shop, and lead their sibling home. This was a tough place to grow up and a tough place to teach.

"Being able to maintain appropriate discipline was the single most valued teaching skill. In truth, all hell could be breaking loose in your classroom, but so long as your kids weren't running through the halls, no one paid much attention (i.e., as long as the school *looked* orderly, everything was fine). Not much attention was given to teaching and learning.

"There were no substantive efforts to build a more positive productive culture. We never gathered to discuss vision or missions or goals. No meetings were held to set priorities. There were no school-wide initiatives to keep improving and no professional development for coordinating curricula or collaborating on instruction. Everyone seemed resigned to just 'getting by' and over time this was demoralizing and debilitating.

"The impact of being immersed in this wearying environment day after day became agonizingly clear to me during a discussion I had with a colleague who had been working in the school for six or seven years. We were chatting in the hallway after dismissal, and I was sharing some thoughts I had for my classes. I guess I was rather animated in talking about my ideas. When I stopped, she didn't comment on my planned lessons, but on my demeanor, my enthusiasm.

"Looking back, I remember that she had a strong academic background and that I thought she was 'smart.' She was personable with a good sense of humor and was a favorite with students. She was the kind of teacher you would assume was doing a terrific job even in this tough neighborhood, and I admired her—that's why what she said next was so disheartening and memorable.

"She told me that she used to be just as enthusiastic as I was—used to feel that she was on a mission to empower the students in her class by imparting skills and knowledge to help them overcome obstacles and succeed in life—but that she didn't feel that way anymore. She said, with clarity and an air of surrender, that she was now a member of '*paychecks personnel*' (her exact words), and that her motivation to teach was now entirely related to receiving a salary.

"The adversity and neglect of the school's working system had caused this teacher's initial positive energy and optimism to dwindle until she gradually became someone 'just going through the motions.' All intrinsic motivation had withered and died. This is what happens to good teachers in a bad system. Systems are important."

We call your attention again to one of W. Edwards Deming's fourteen recommendations for organizations—"Find and eliminate barriers to pride in workmanship." As a part of your systems analysis, periodically ask your staff if there are practices within the school's operations that make it difficult for them to fulfill their mission of doing what is best for students.

Counterproductive processes should not be the subject of disruptive "water cooler complaining"; instead, they call for a legitimate forum that will provide an opportunity for such practices to be fixed. When a staff examines its educational system component by component, and acts collaboratively over time to strengthen the curriculum and build effective teaching practices, that is *systems thinking* in action.

Phase IV, Step 6: Get out of the bunker. It is quite easy for a principal, or any leader, to become office-bound, scheduling back-to-back meetings and doing all the prep and follow-up for them. The ensuing complaint is, "I just can't get out of my office." We think it is essential for the leader to get out of his or her office and into the areas where the organization's operations take place.

Observing what is happening firsthand is a form of measurement. Experiencing and observing real-time operations contributes powerfully to the leader's ability to accurately assess the need for adjustments or new objectives.

Being visible and accessible imparts other benefits to a leader: Moving around the building connects administrators with their workforce. It's hard to create teamwork and a sense of working together if there is a separation in the mind of employees between "the office" and what is happening "out here in the trenches." When a leader is rarely seen, it prompts an "us and them" mentality.

Another reason to "get out there" is to promote a "4:1 or 5:1" positive environment as we have mentioned. How can we determine what to compliment or encourage if we don't get out of the office? In his book *Bringing Out the Best in People*, Dr. Aubrey Daniels cites research that the best managers spend more time in the work area because it makes for the most effective delivery of positive reinforcement.

We help to create a positive environment (in a home, classroom, or workplace), when we offer supportive and encouraging remarks four or five times as often as critical or corrective comments. This balance earns leadership the characterization of being understanding and supportive, while the corrective "1," if it is done right, then tends to be received as reasonable and fair. Amassing the 4:1 or 5:1 ratio is achieved by observing and noting the good work people are doing and the energy they are investing.

During your "walkabouts," don't rush; being a willing and patient listener counts as a part of building a 4:1 environment. The time we give to others speaks loudly about our respect for them and the value we place on hearing what they have to say.

Nels and Joe: "Carolyn Davis, principal emeritus of Ipswich's other elementary school (the Winthrop School), with whom we worked for twelve years, did an amazing job at building the 5:1 environment. She encouraged and showed appreciation with great sincerity that came across in the most positive way. She was truly present and attentive in every conversation. When talking with her, you sensed her listening empathetically to understand your views. Instead of interpreting your thoughts just from her own perspective, she endeavored to get her mind into your world. As a result, she built a great wellspring of trust, mutual respect, and support that enabled her to take on the occasional hard issue without losing the positive culture.

"Regardless of age or level of professionalism, it feels great to be noticed and appreciated!

"Pay attention to the positive things others are doing and let them know that you have seen and sincerely appreciate their efforts. If you can, write a note and put some of your comments into a bigger, vision context like 'you made a positive contribution to the life of the school' or 'you made a difference for students.' This elevates the level of your comments by attaching purpose and idealism, which is a very powerful form of encouragement."

So how do you make the time to get around your building? The same way you make time for improvement planning, *you put it in the schedule.* Put aside an hour or more every day to visit classrooms, observe teachers, read to a class, teach a lesson, or just walk around and talk to people about how their jobs are going. Consider that time as you would an important appointment, not to be canceled except for emergencies.

Nels: "I was involved in a lot of supervisor training and evaluation in industry. Here's an important tip when you evaluate your staff: If you see a problem, don't let it slide; don't take the easy way out. After seeing the many difficulties caused by known but ignored problems, I began to ask supervisors if they would 'let their children play in the traffic.' They would look at me with a puzzled look and say, 'Of course not.' Then I would add, 'Isn't it the same thing when you let someone you supervise, someone who depends on you for leadership, carry on with poor practices because you haven't mustered the courage to tell them the truth?'

"Those poor practices are likely to cause them to 'get run over' on the job. It is my experience that flawed practices, left unmentioned by supervisors, get worse; sooner or later they cause problems that damage the organization and may well end up costing that person's job."

While walking around your building, *avoid using your presence to micromanage.* You will send the wrong message (and staff may start to close their doors when they see you coming). That doesn't mean that you should ignore that which needs improvement. Take a stand on working values, good teaching practices, and what is "best for students"; but in most cases you don't need to *instantly* address those concerns either. Don't take on "tough issues" on the spot in a rush to get them corrected. With adults as with students, it's best to praise in public and correct in private. Invest some thoughtfulness coming up with the right language, the right time, and the right place for corrective comments.

Be firm, but remain on the person's side, separating the person from the issue by sticking firmly to the issue in an impersonal way. This makes you a steady, reliable presence in your building.

Phase IV, Step 7: Let teachers be program builders.

Ken: "We wanted to teach our students how to use prior knowledge, inferential reasoning, and questioning techniques to enhance their reading experience and deepen understanding. We found we could not purchase a commercial comprehension skills curriculum that aligned with our specific instructional objectives. We concluded that it would be best if we selected materials from a variety of sources and then developed our own courses specifically tailored to our instructional objectives—and to our students' tastes, needs, and abilities.

"We kept the reading text we had, using it as a convenient literature anthology, and each grade collected and compiled the additional reading selections we would need to teach the reading comprehension skills we were targeting.

"We view teachers as collaborators in creating the most engaging curriculum; anything less than that ignores the importance of felt-need on the part of both the teacher and the student.

"A first-year teacher arrives in his or her new school as a result of the cumulative flow of a long series of decisions they have made. The new teacher is then immediately immersed into a well-defined and ubiquitous power hierarchy analogous to what you would expect to find in the military: school committee, superintendent, assistant superintendent, curriculum coordinator, principals and assistant principals, followed by teachers, assistants, and volunteers. School organizations draw tight parameters around who gets to decide what.

"Teachers arrive as decision makers and then, as if their thoughtfulness and judgment were no longer skills pertinent to their new job, are often boss-managed and told what to do. There are exceptions, but this is often the 'default' nature of public school systems according to what I have seen—and it will remain so unless visionary leaders (perhaps like you?) come along to coax the system in a direction that makes more sense.

"Otherwise it is likely that key aspects of the school's operations that are crucial to a teacher's professional effectiveness will reside mostly outside their sphere of influence."

Phase IV, Step 8: Break deadlocks and overcome roadblocks. Expect disagreement. Don't be torn apart by it, don't become stalemated; just work it through. When there is disagreement, back up the group by asking, "Where do we agree on this and where is it that we have disagreement? Let's break down the differences and see what we can do with them." Use a calm, objective voice; the leader's tone sets the tone for the group. Understand that it is not the leader's job to pull back control when the going gets sticky, but rather to work with the group to ensure that it becomes unstuck. With appropriate modeling, over time, the group will learn how to work its way through any problem situation that may arise.

Encourage those who are focused on "don't wants" to share what it is they "do want." Ask the group to state their aims in the affirmative. Work with the group to develop a range of options for goals or solutions. Ensure that the options are discussed until one is chosen—at least for a pilot or trial.

If discussion participants stick to the following, they have every chance of reaching consensus:

- staying focused on the issue;
- looking forward to the solution;
- avoiding personal comment and blame;
- transparently searching for the best option;
- getting all the facts out on the table;
- objectively examining pros and cons so the best ideas have a chance to "rise to the surface"; and
- listening to fully grasp the underlying core beliefs of others.

Keep these factors in mind as you observe staff participating in the planning process. Adhering to these guidelines will ease your group toward resolution of issues while minimizing the likelihood of roadblocks and deadlocks from occurring in the first place.

Use "reflective listening" and "I statements." Reflective listening Reflective listening means listening to others with the deep intent of understanding their thinking, rather than taking the focus back to yourself by offering other solutions, counterarguments, or critical comments, or by completely changing the topic.

An "*I statement*" is an explanation of how you feel, made only from your point of view, without reference to others that will cause them to become defensive. Listen first reflectively, strive to understand all the facts and emotions, then share how you see things in the form of an "I statement." Avoid "you" statements at all cost. We can't read other people's minds, and blaming just results in close-minded defensiveness. In the end, what others need from us is to know what *we* think and what *we* feel, not what we think *they* are thinking, or how we interpret their motives. Let them speak for themselves.

Ken: "*The best way to avoid deadlocks and roadblocks is to preclude them.* A collaborative environment, with working values in place, and the right balance of empowerment and alignment, helps to avoid deadlocks and roadblocks. It is not an ounce, but a pound of prevention.

"*Be alert to shifts in cultural tone,* while making sure that your words and deeds are having a positive effect. Monitor your own actions carefully. A mistake I made some years back is a good example: A staff member came to my office and told me that I had hurt her feelings by quickly dismissing a suggestion she made at a recent staff meeting. Upon reflection, she was right—this occurrence could have discouraged her future participation had she not had the courage to come to my office and clear the air. After this incident I resolved to keep a sharper eye out for any of my own actions that might have a chilling effect on the process."

Examine your environment with an objective eye. Determine if your employees feel it is a safe environment—one where they are not only encouraged to be creative and to contribute to making a better organization, but one where they feel free and secure in doing so.

Joe: *"Another important dynamic to watch out for are instances of 'emotional hijacking.'* Author Daniel Goleman, in his seminal book *Emotional Intelligence*, popularized the term in his review of emerging brain research. Three negative actions of the brain's emotional system—inaccuracy, illogical thought, and escalation of problems—can occur when a person is in what we call 'emotions-only mode.' The comparative and more objective services of the cortex and its frontal lobe are not a part of the person's thinking or behavior at that moment. Emotionally charged moments are an occasion for alert leaders to model calmness, encourage respectfulness, remind participants of the working values, and if necessary suggest that the group back up to common ground or take a break!

"The job of the leader is to pull negativity out of the process, so that progress can flow freely; it certainly isn't a leader's job to add negativity. I am not suggesting that you accept disrespect or ignore violations of the working values. Call people on disrespectful behavior, remind them about the working values, but do it in a way that addresses the behavior—in a calm but firm way—without making negative comments about the person. People will be looking to the leader to be a calming influence on the group and to help them refocus in times of stress. Your job is to keep your culture on track, and when it seems to be going 'off the rails,' to quickly lead them back to a good place.

"In a recent conversation, Sheila Conley, the current principal of the Doyon School, commented to me that she has never been a part of an organization where the staff was so professional in the way they approached solving problems. She sent a note to Ken, complimenting him on the development of such a culture. Ken was thrilled that the professional culture of the school was still going strong and that it was sufficiently noticeable to prompt such a comment."

A safe, open, and positive work environment, characterized by good communication, is our greatest ally in precluding and preventing deadlocks and roadblocks.

We developed the diagram in figure 6.2 to depict the kind of balance that we want our organization to achieve. When we are empathetic, respectful, and protective of each other's rights, we avoid aggressive and passive-aggressive behaviors. The key to getting a job done well with high morale is to keep our focus on *outstanding service to students*; in so doing, personal ambitions, territorial disputes, and all other lesser aims take a back seat."

Even if the quality of our environment is topnotch, we will still encounter periodic disagreements and potential disputes. When these inevitable "disturbances in the force" come our way, how do we handle them? An initial positive mindset is crucial; while you can expect disagreements to occur, you

A Framework for Workplace Relationships

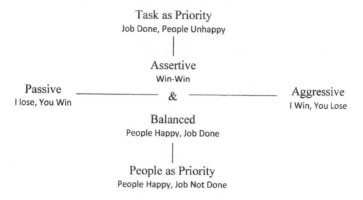

Task as Priority
Job Done, People Unhappy

Assertive
Win-Win

Passive ——————— & ——————— Aggressive
I lose, You Win   I Win, You Lose

Balanced
People Happy, Job Done

People as Priority
People Happy, Job Not Done

Interpersonal Style:

Passive = Someone who does not stand up for their own rights.
Aggressive = Someone who pursues their own rights at the expense of the rights of others.
Assertive = Someone who advocates for their own rights while protecting the rights of others.

Priority Focus:

Task Priority = Highest priority is getting the job done.
People Priority = Highest priority is relating well to people.
Balanced Priority = Getting the job done while nurturing positive relationships.

Figure 6.2.   A Framework for Workplace Relationships

must also believe in the group's ability to get past the trouble spots. Urge your teams to alert you as soon as a problem is perceived. As you start to look into the problem, consider first the "positioning" of the contending parties, rather than the particulars of the issue in contention (refer to figure 5.1, "Problem-Solving Positions").

The best initial approach for resolving deadlocks and roadblocks is to

• *restore respect, and*
• *reset positions, so that people are looking at the problem together.*

When resolving a dispute, you may need to grapple initially (and separately from the facts at issue) with the problem of not standing together, personal blaming, or instances of disrespectful actions or speech. Temporarily stop focusing on the issue and work to clear up the disrespect or lack of common perspective. Address in the same way any lack of truthfulness, lack of cooperation, or any action that is a violation of trust. The same goes for violations of the working values that insert negative emotions or defensiveness into the dialogue. Listen for tenor and tone; listen for contentiousness; clear the personal stuff out of the way first. Separating the personal from the problem is the biggest and most important step in breaking deadlocks.

Train your staff to focus forward on the issues and solutions.

Reset positions by gently reminding all contending parties—anyone engaged in blame, disrespect, or the like—that we are all here to accomplish gains for our students, and that disputes within the team are counterproductive to that end. Being drawn into the particulars of a dispute often causes us to forget the bigger picture.

Reasserting the vision and the need for unity is a good way to soften or end disputes. The particulars of a dispute tend to look small when measured against the importance of our larger goals, particularly the well-being of students.

Part of our vision is to work successfully together under the working values in a way that leads to high job satisfaction. Reaffirm that aspiration as well. If hints and gentle reminders fail, ask the group to take a firm stand in reasserting that purpose. When poor positioning is cleared away, when the respectful character of our culture is restored, we can proceed to try to resolve the issue that is before the group.

You are in an appropriate position to begin solving a problem when you have first cleared away blame, fear, disrespect, defensiveness, lack of trust, lack of cooperation, and any violation of the working values.

In problem-solving brainstorms or planning discussions, don't allow disparaging comments about ideas to be offered. Delay comments as to merit or "favorites," until after generating pros and cons and doing a quick prioritization. Ideas with limited merit will drop off the list of options without anyone having to directly disparage another person's ideas. Use prioritization to avoid confrontations and hurt feelings.

People don't like it when others disparage their ideas, but they will generally be accepting if it is the judgment of the group that other ideas have more value than theirs at this time, especially if the group arrived at the judgment through an objective, impersonal process.

A staff member's failure to live up to a collective agreement (i.e., after consensus has been reached), is another potential area for contentiousness.

What do you do when someone on the staff doesn't appear to be complying with a working value or a curricular consensus established by the group? We suggest you take the following three steps in sequence.

1. *Check the decision being challenged for possible flaws or needed adjustments.* If appropriate, ask the group if others are having problems in this

particular area. Hearing the group's position, the offending person might self-correct. If others are having the same problem, consider appointing an ad hoc committee to investigate and offer insight and options.

2. *Provide a private listening session.* Meet with the individual and privately seek to understand his or her reasons for failing to adhere to the norm. If you can help sort out the issue, you may be able to obtain voluntary compliance as opposed to having to go right to "enforcement." It is always best to obtain *a person's voluntary self-initiated change* if possible.

3. *Tell the person (or persons) they must adhere to the norm.* If the above two approaches fail to produce the needed change, then the responsibilities of leadership require you to tell the person to adhere to the consensus norm. We cannot allow behaviors to continue that undermine the group's decisions; to do so would render those decisions meaningless. Once the issues have been prioritized, the options have been clarified, and everyone has had an opportunity to participate in the discussions and offer their perspective, and once consensus has been reached, everyone is expected to get "on board" and give their best "good faith" effort to make the plan a success. When the group has spoken, it is done. No "lone gulls" permitted—to do otherwise is to allow the process to be sabotaged.

If someone adopts a blocking position, recognize that the potential conflict is not with you personally, but with the school's vision, or goals and objectives, all of which have been decided by consensus and are meant to do "what is best for kids." Pit blockers against the vision or goals, not yourself, and let that guide your actions.

Whether you are dealing with a failure to comply or the assumption of a blocking position, these behaviors are the reason there is a "1" in the "5:1" rule. It is not the "5:0" rule. Corrective actions are a part of building a great organization and are necessary; otherwise our failure to correct is a tacit agreement that harmful words or actions are acceptable.

A "mutually exclusive" decision may create a deadlock. Ours is a consensus process. Voting should be infrequent, but at times it may be necessary. If, after using the problem-solving process and fully pursuing all viewpoints there is a mutually exclusive choice, you may have to vote. This is a situation where we can do A or B but cannot reconcile them. If the majority wants B, and have explored why the proponents of A are holding firm, and there is no way to make an A/B combination, or find a good third option, then we are left with a "mutually exclusive choice." The process could become deadlocked by such a situation.

We previously mentioned that we recommend a sufficiency of vote of 75 percent of those present in such instances. The percentage of that sufficiency of vote should be decided in advance as a part of your meeting rules (e.g., "If we have to vote, and 75 percent are on-board, then we move ahead"). Be very mindful that leaving substantial minorities behind by out-voting them may plant the seeds of future discord or failure. Don't be afraid when the voting plurality is below 75 percent to continue to search for a better solution or further clarification of issues and motivations. On the other hand, being deadlocked, losing momentum and motivation, having the process seen as ineffectual, is deadly. This is particularly the case on an issue that requires taking action. So work very hard for consensus, but vote occasionally when you must.

Phase IV, Step 9: Display and celebrate progress. Data is motivating. Find creative ways to compile and display data that motivates and energizes. A good example, albeit a bit dated, is the thermometer chart showing the progress of a fund drive. It visualizes a hope that the fundraising will reach its goal. During a reading marathon, the Doyon School used a paper snake, each new section representing a substantial number of additional minutes read by students, to display and motivate. The students kept reading and the snake kept growing until it wound its way through the entire school. People like visuals; they motivate us to act.

Whenever selecting a new goal or objective, be sure to immediately consider ways of measuring and displaying progress. Measure right away at the start, so that in a year or two everyone will be able to see how far we've come. Try to find a colorful, motivating way to display the progress you are measuring. If your chosen approach to measuring and displaying isn't stimulating interest or action, get creative and find a more motivating way to display progress that does catch the imagination. When you give teams their charge, in the written description of what they are expected to do, include the expectation that they obtain baseline data right away and at intervals thereafter measure and display progress.

When a group that is committed to continuous improvement merely hears an idea they like, things begin to change in their classrooms. That has been a surprise to us. By the time a goal is finalized, its T's crossed and I's dotted, the train of progress is already going down the tracks. It's been amazing how fast good stuff can start happening. Don't be surprised when the goal is finalized and they say, "We've already made a lot of progress on that." If we don't measure early on, we are likely to miss the true baseline.

View goals and objectives as destinations. For each destination, consider the route to get there. As a leader you are facilitating the process of the group as they travel that route. Choose a few locations along the way that have a sense of achievement to celebrate as milestones. Recognize effort. Honor what different individuals or groups did to help get to the milestone, and be specific in offering praise. This type of modeling is powerful. Those within earshot will want to be part of getting to the next milestone and will ascertain what it takes to get there.

What is noticed and applauded will be repeated.

Look for opportunities to mark collaborative successes with some unexpected collaborative fun. There is nothing wrong with accompanying good news or goal accomplishment with a surprise ice cream sundae party, a pizza lunch, or the next staff meeting held at the local miniature golf course. Dr. Aubrey Daniels cautions us bluntly that a vision that does not include a plan for celebrating will fail to motivate.

Don't be afraid to submit news of accomplishments or achievements to media outlets, be they related to students, faculty, or parents. If parents construct some new play equipment or donate new technology, take pictures, make a video; put these on local cable outlets, in the newspaper, and on the Internet.

But avoid "braggy" prediction types of things, along the lines of "Here are the great things we're *going* to do." *We don't want to encourage the group to celebrate its own bragging, but to celebrate real achievement.* Words are easy. Our position should always be one of under-promising and over-delivering. Accomplishment is credibility; it builds motivation and unity.

Phase IV, Step 10: Review and renew goals and objectives. At least once a year, there should be an official dialogue about how we are progressing and whether we need to make changes to our goals, even if it is not a full-blown goals/objectives review with a complete list of questions. This is true even if you have a two-year cycle as we did at the Doyon School. The annual review is also an appropriate time to update other building principals and central office administrators as to the status of the school's initiatives so they can offer support and provide input.

If in the process of an interim review the conversation widens with discussion emerging of possible changes, then switch plans and go through the process more fully. Resist efforts to add additional long-term goals *during* the year and especially impulsively even if someone offers a seemingly good idea. Long-term goal possibilities must go into the queue. Once you have carefully selected the goals and objectives most worthy of your time and effort, that's it, until an objective becomes fully realized and operational. At that point (even in the middle of the year) the group can choose another goal or objective from the queue.

Avoid informally adding goals and objectives "outside of the process"; doing so will invite burnout, loss of focus, and ineffectiveness.

To help you identify which types of initiatives may be successfully added during the year on top of your main improvement plan goals, we provide the following descriptors.

- *Informational-Level Planning*—consists of sharing information to foster improvement. It takes only the time to share the information. As long as this is not overly time consuming, and requires no schedule changes or resource allocation, it can be done at any time.

- *Low-Level Planning*—calls for the creation of a plan, but only requires one or two meetings, uses existing resources, resolves new or unexpected problems, and requires no major schedule changes. Initiatives of this sort can be taken at any time with approval of the group.
- *High-Level Planning*—requires multiple meetings and widespread participation, may involve new resources or shifting of resources, and can involve schedule changes. Such planning must go in the queue and not be added to the planning workload except through the goal selection process, when there is an opening. Emergencies are of course an exception.

A REVIEW OF CHAPTER 6 CONCEPTS

- A commitment to continuous improvement is the third ingredient in creating cycles of success; when added to teamwork and focused goal setting, ongoing achievement is produced.
- Only change a broad directional vision or goal when it no longer reflects your priorities. When individual goals and objectives are accomplished, replace them with your next highest priorities.
- To keep the improvement dialogue going, engage in a periodic discussion of questions about how we are doing and where we want to go next.
- Allow teachers to be a part of the hiring process; it will result in a stronger team.
- Let teachers be a part of designing and building the curriculum; it makes for a stronger curriculum.
- Value data. We are where we are, we can either know it or not.
- Surveys are a valuable part of the flow of data. Review the sample survey questions in appendix I.
- A successful outcome is the result of well-conceived planning and problem-solving processes. Review the processes in appendix H.
- Find the "barriers to pride in workmanship" that exist in your school and systematically eliminate them.
- Don't be office-bound. Get into the corridors and classrooms.
- Don't let anybody outdo you in noticing and commenting on the good things your staff is doing.
- Be alert to shifts in cultural tone; examine your environment with an objective eye.
- When a controversy breaks out, (1) restore respect, and (2) reset positions so that the group is standing together looking at the problem.
- Do not allow behaviors to continue that undermine the group's decisions.
- Display progress creatively and celebrate the achievement of milestones.

- Review goals and objectives periodically, asking, " *In what ways can we do more to help students acquire the skills, absorb the knowledge, and understand the concepts that they will need to succeed in life in the twenty-first century?* "

Conclusion

Renewing Your School's Educational Systems

Creating a great school requires working from the foundation up: We begin by observing the school's educational systems; and then, working together over time, we renew and revitalize these systems piece by piece, resulting in a stronger, more effective, extraordinary school.

There is no substitute for

- widespread ownership of improvements;
- the ability to work together effectively;
- a powerful flow of creative improvement ideas;
- consensus unity behind vision and goals;
- the reconstruction of both culture and curriculum brick by brick;
- the development of high-quality materials and instructional programs;
- effort and thoroughness generated by enthusiastic implementation;
- an ongoing commitment to progress year in and year out; and
- a consistent, priority commitment to what is best for students.

There is no pill to take, no wholesale replacement of staff, or any external decree that will transform a failing, average, or good school into an extraordinary one. If we tear down an old school, combine schools, build a new facility, create a new charter school, negotiate a new contract, or anything else, *success will still depend on the quality of the working culture and educational systems functioning within that school.*

We do not believe in silver bullets, but rather in the hard work of continuous improvement—an incremental process that calls upon the staff of a school to work collaboratively, in a sustainable way, while building ever-improving educational systems. Though it is hard work, it is not an onerous task, but a rewarding, deeply meaningful, and most enjoyable thing to do.

If we start there (i.e., if we rebuild the American educational system school by school from the inside out), the buildings may continue to look the same from the outside, but inside the educational programs will be ready to prepare our students for the challenges of the twenty-first century.

Joe: "In this sometimes hard-bitten, sarcastic world a mutually held dream of continuous improvement can come across to the modern ear as 'sappy.' Give yourself permission to be 'sappy'; let your dreams live and not die from fear of failure or disapproval before they are born. It is the 'sappy dreamers'—people with a *vision*, 'sappy' yet tinged with pragmatism and wisdom—who bring the really good things of this world to life."

Nels: "Let go of viewing leadership as being about 'control.' Free yourself to lead an empowering process of continuous improvement. You may think the principal/leader has to have control. Control is truly an illusion. Your job as a leader is to (1) find the most creative, effective solutions that will make a difference for students and (2) see that those solutions are implemented with the enthusiasm required for their dynamic success.

Ask yourself what seeking the most creative, effective solutions—and seeing that they are implemented with enthusiasm—has to do with personal control.

Not a lot, we would say. All the notion of personal control does is get in your way. Let go, become the process facilitator, and let collaboration lead the way. Dare to believe in your staff. Dare to believe in continuous improvement. Dare to believe in your ability to lead an engaging, living process—to become a leader of leaders. It is the finest form of leadership available today."

Ken: "A couple of years into our process, 'consistency' emerged as a goal at the Doyon School. The emergence of 'consistency' as an overarching goal was momentous for a number of reasons. First, it lent legitimacy to what was to become an ongoing sequential process of examining different areas of our curriculum (the order decided by the faculty) through the lens of consistency. Secondly, it represented an implicit commitment on each teacher's part to pass on to the following year's teachers children who had been taught using the consensus-identified curricula and methods.

In a sense it was a commitment to 'unselfishness.' The focus on consistency represented a most powerful shift: the relinquishing of a school run by a loose conglomeration of individual goals in favor of a school run by group collaboration—*it was a move from a 'self-centered' perspective to a 'student-serving' focus.*

Education is a team sport. Each set of teachers prepares the student for next year's teachers; the quality of the product—the graduate—is a team achievement."

In education we are working on behalf of a truly noble cause. Every day they are right there in front of us, the students whose lives we affect. All we need is a system for working that is worthy of the work—a system that recognizes and harnesses the idealistic visions and inherent energies that brought us to the profession in the first place.

The intent of this book is to help you create that type of system in your school. Throughout the book we have tried to show you how to build good teamwork, how to activate intrinsic motivation, and how to use the focused energy produced to generate ongoing cycles of improvement—all for the benefit of your students. Over time, this process will transform your school. In so doing it is also likely to bring the joy of accomplishment into your life. We wish you great success on your journey *toward becoming a great school.*

Appendix A

A Guide to Effective Meetings

MEETING ROLES

The assignment of roles is critical to having an effective meeting. Those assuming the roles provide key functions necessary for the meeting to go smoothly. Roles can be combined at smaller meetings. For example, at meetings of five or fewer persons, roles could be reduced to a facilitator/gatekeeper and a timekeeper/notetaker. At larger meetings all roles should be assigned.

Leader

- may or may not attend the meeting;
- helps set the schedule of meetings;
- makes sure the team is focused on the process steps;
- helps define objectives and the processes used to attain them;
- provides necessary training;
- receives regular reports and minutes; and
- helps the process move past deadlocks and roadblocks.

The leader is often chosen by the team, except where the full faculty sits as a team and the principal fills the leadership role. The leader ensures that the team's charge is clear and if necessary clarifies the team's mission. The leader initiates the process by calling the first meeting to determine the process steps. The leader and the coordinating team prepare process steps for discussion by the full team. Between meetings, the leader follows the progress of subteams to ensure that upcoming meetings of the full team will be productive. The leader also checks that minutes are kept. The leader ensures that resources needed by the team are made available. Depending on skills and the circumstance, the leader may also serve as facilitator.

Facilitator

- chairs meetings and is responsible for the agenda;
- receives input regarding the agenda;
- ensures that roles are assigned;
- reminds all members of the working values and team rules;
- keeps the meeting focused on the agenda;
- stops digressions;
- begins and ends meetings on time;
- is familiar with the process steps and tools;
- ensures open, balanced participation;
- breaks agenda items down into subcomponents as the need arises;
- goes around the group for input at critical junctures;
- helps break deadlocks;
- obtains some clear resolution of the agenda item before moving on;
- understands and works for consensus;
- works to understand the basis for competing views; finds core motivating factors;
- is responsible for counting voting pluralities; and
- is neutral about decision outcomes.

The facilitator arranges seating so that members can see each other and have a surface to write on. If the group is large, a small bell or gavel should be available. The facilitator may conduct "Thank You" time at the start of a meeting to build group cohesion and morale. The facilitator ensures that agenda items are of interest to the whole group while less important or time consuming items are considered first by a subgroup.

It is important for the facilitator to keep the discussion at the proper level (i.e., when the group is engaged in deciding *what* to do, making sure that they don't digress into *how* to do it). If helpful, the facilitator breaks a topic down into components to keep the discussion from becoming scattered. The facilitator should recognize those who wish to speak. Side conversations should be discouraged in a kind but firm way.

Going around the group one person at a time is an important option that should be used to encourage broad participation when deliberating important issues. Discussion in large groups can be broken out into subgroups of three to five, with each subgroup reporting on specific findings or ideas. The occasional nonbinding show of hands can be used to informally assess group sentiment.

After a brainstorming session, ideas offered by individuals should be prioritized to find which options elicit the broadest interest. Group time should not be used to discuss suggestions that have little support—the level of support ought to be assessed first. At the start of a meeting the facilitator describes for the group what he or she hopes will be accomplished, and at the end briefly reviews what progress has been made. Agenda items ought to be brought to a conclusion (e.g., postponed to another meeting, delayed for more facts, referred to a subgroup, or approved or rejected).

Gatekeeper/Assistant Facilitator

- observes the participation and flow of the meeting;
- encourages participation, particularly from quieter members;
- stops domineering behavior;
- monitors the discussion for violations of working values or meeting rules;
- keeps the meeting from becoming repetitive;
- suggests refocusing when discussion becomes scattered;
- helps the meeting break deadlocks;
- understands and works for consensus; and
- takes over for the facilitator if necessary.

The gatekeeper supports the facilitator by providing assistance with participation, staying on topic, and moving issues along. He or she should not be shy about speaking up to help the meeting stay focused. When the gatekeeper notices the discussion reaching the point of repetition or digression, he or she may ask the facilitator if that is the case. If, for example, the discussion unexpectedly turns to where to put the new soda machine, the gatekeeper should say something. If the facilitator is strong and experienced, however, the gatekeeper may not have a lot to do. The gatekeeper is a full participant in the discussion. The gatekeeper's comments and suggestions are always made with tact and respect.

Timekeeper

- encourages starting the meeting on time;
- makes sure speakers keep to time allotments on the agenda;
- establishes the beginning and end of breaks;
- issues alerts before time runs out on an agenda item;
- asks if the members want to extend time on an item or for the meeting; and
- helps the meeting to end on time.

The timekeeper watches the meeting carefully to see that it begins and ends on time. An alert should be issued to the facilitator a few minutes before the assigned time for an item expires. The group can then decide if it wants to continue working on the item, or carry the item over to the next meeting and move on to the next agenda item. The facilitator decides with member approval or asks the members to decide if they want to extend the time.

Notetaker

- keeps minutes during the meeting;
- records who is present;
- records the beginning and ending times;
- does not record everything said but notes which topics were discussed;
- records all votes and decisions;
- prepares and circulates copies of the minutes;
- maintains a file of minutes; and
- helps keep a file of charts, lists, etc., developed at meetings.

In discussions, members are encouraged to be creative and candid. They should know that the minutes will not record every idea offered or statement made. That would inhibit creativity and candor. The most important things to be included in the minutes are the decisions the team makes.

Visual Materials Organizer

- is assigned as needed;
- organizes charts, overheads, projection materials, etc.;
- records brainstorming contributions, prioritizing results, etc., on whatever media is being used for all to see;
- makes sure that what is recorded is understood and that ideas are not lost;
- helps the facilitator keep track of visual materials created by the group; and
- compiles results from visual materials and provides results to the notetaker.

Technology Organizer

- advises leader/facilitator as to uses of technology;
- tests equipment before the meeting;
- operates equipment during the meeting; and
- disassembles and stores the technology equipment used at the meeting.

Team Members

- arrive on time and prepared;
- listen to each other;
- put aside personal agendas in deference to the team's mission;
- observe the working values in and out of meetings; and
- work toward consensus.

All team members are leaders in the way that they conduct themselves and set the example for others.

Issues should be discussed with gusto, but once the team reaches consensus, all members need to put aside previous views and enthusiastically support the group's decision. To do otherwise is to sabotage the mission of the group. A few persons should not be allowed to hold the group back or passively undermine the plan once their views have been given a full airing and it is clear that most of the group wants to move forward in a different direction.

Team Guidelines

At the first meeting, a team or ongoing committee should establish a set of rules or guidelines for its own functioning. Rules help members to understand each other's preferences and sensitivities. They help meetings to run smoothly and efficiently.

Examples of Guidelines

- Submit suggestions for the agenda to the facilitator.
- Let the facilitator know if you will not be attending.
- Arrive on time.
- Bring all needed materials.
- Arrange for someone to be in charge of beverages or other refreshments at meetings.
- No agenda, no meeting.
- Start and stop on time.
- Working values are in effect at all meetings.
- Speak one at a time, once recognized by the facilitator.
- Stay on topic.
- Use pros and cons to compare options.
- Listen carefully and acknowledge the good points in others' ideas.
- Decision making is by consensus.
- If an item goes to a vote it requires a 75 percent plurality to pass.
- Take ten-minute breaks every hour.

THE AGENDA FORMAT

Except for brief informal gatherings, all meetings should have an agenda with elements similar to those included in the sample below.

It is important to make every effort to resolve an agenda item before moving on. That could mean either deciding to continue the discussion at another meeting, rescheduling to wait for further information, or voting to approve or reject the item. The important point is to conclude the item with a degree of clarity that everyone understands.

DATE: October 4
TIME: 2:30–4:00 PM
PLACE: Library
PREPARATION: Bring recommendations and notes
OBJECTIVE: Develop goals for improvement

Topics	Process	Person	Time
1. Introductions	around group	leader	5 min.
2. Thank you time	acknowledge work accomplished	leader et al.	5 min
3. First item	visiting expert	Mr. Smith	15 min.
4. Second item	subcommittee report	Ben	15 min.
5. Third item	goal discussion	leader	40 min.
6. New business		any member	5 min.

Appendix B

A Guide to Consensus

In our view, consensus occurs when all the necessary information is in, when we have evaluated all available options, and when almost everyone sees that one of the options is clearly the best we can do at this time. Consensus is not when everybody thinks the leading option is perfect, just the best we can do at this time.

If 20–40 percent of the group doesn't agree with the other 60–80 percent, we need to root out why they feel that way. Two possibilities worth considering are (1) the group feels they need more information or options; and (2) there is a stubborn underlying issue at the root of the opposition viewpoint not accounted for in the plan.

Knowing when we have enough information to make a decision requires careful judgment; decisions sometimes are "put out to study" because of the feeling that there *may* be more relevant information. *To not decide is at the least to decide to delay.* If concrete and specific information is needed, then wait; if delaying a tough decision is because of a vague sense that *maybe* there is more information, try to break the logjam.

A perspective that can sometimes free up a gridlocked process is the recognition that this is the best we can do now and that we can modify it later if more information comes along or if changes are required; that is, if the decision lends itself to later modification. There are many types of changes amenable to a "tryout" or limited pilot during which we can test a decision. We get to move ahead by agreeing to try our lead options in one or two classrooms or grades or for a limited period, after which we can assess the results. A trial of the leading option is a good way to break logjams.

Deciding when to move on and when to wait requires thoughtful judgment and objectivity. If you sense that discussions are moving toward additional substantive options, encourage the group to continue. If not, and if it is your sense that all meaningful options are already "on the table," encourage the group to reach closure. As a way to begin to move toward closure, ask the staff if they feel that they have considered all meaningful options.

Consensus means that time has been provided for the issues to be fully discussed, the pros and cons have been fully explored, everyone has had an opportunity to weigh in, and *at least 75 percent feel that a particular action is the best we can do at this time.* Work hard for 100 percent support, but when differences can't be fully reconciled, there still needs to be a minimum of 75 percent in favor of going ahead. The percentage of the group that wants to move ahead needs to be high; do not leave substantial minorities behind; it will come back to haunt the process in the future.

A KEY TO CONSENSUS: SEARCHING FOR "CORE MOTIVATING TRUTHS"

Joe: "A few years ago our family held a reunion celebrating 100 years since my grandfather and his brothers came to America. We expected 250 people at the event—all cousins. There was lots of enthusiasm; it was going well until at a committee meeting, the issue of how the food would be provided threatened to split the group. The majority felt we should cook the food ourselves as that was the style of the founding families we were honoring— and that the cost of catering would be too much of a financial imposition on young families.

"There was a substantial minority, however, who wanted the event to be catered because some relatives were too old to help cook for a large group. This group also felt that that option would leave more time for socializing. When the discussion started to get divisive, we delayed the food decision to the next meeting, and went on with other items. The meeting broke up with a negative undercurrent.

"After the meeting, I walked out with my cousin Tom, who had spoken most passionately for the group that wanted catering. It took twenty minutes of probing conversation about catering and people's preferences before the key motivating factor came out. Tom said that when we had the last big family reunion, he remembered that the various families prepared their own food and ate in their own separate clusters. He felt it greatly reduced the amount of interfamily socialization. *This* was the source of the passion driving his strong stand. It turned out that his 'core motivating truth' was not a problem but in fact a point around which we could forge a solution.

"One of the goals the committee had already agreed upon was to bring everyone closer together as a family. At the next meeting we started out with Tom's underlying concern, which immediately pulled the two differing groups back together. Beginning at that place, we were able to forge a solution. It was decided that all foods would be prepared for a common buffet that was to be eaten together; that those who wished to cook could do so, and those who wished not to cook could make a donation that would be used to buy additional prepared food for the buffet.

"The food was fabulous, everyone had a great time, and the day ended with us united as a family. We were fortunate to discover that underlying the disagreement was a common motivation that could bridge differences.

"Once one side of a disagreement becomes aware that the other side is motivated by something they too see as important, the dispute can be bridged."

Nels: "When I worked in human resources for GTE/Sylvania I remember an occasion when I was sent to visit a plant that was having labor troubles. They could not get the new contract settled with the union. During my career I had some excellent mentors who gave me a great deal of good advice. One such piece of advice was to always look beneath the surface for underlying issues when disputes are not being resolved.

"With that in mind, I went to the factory floor and talked casually with workers I knew from past visits—not about the contract, just gabbing about how things were at the plant. It turned out the real issue was a feeling among the women in the plant that the managing foreman didn't treat them equally compared to the men. I realized that because of the unhappiness of the women, there was too much in-fighting in the union to ever allow them to agree to any contract. The negotiations were in gridlock and the real issue wasn't even part of the discussion.

"After talking with me, the plant general manager called in the managing foreman, read him the riot act, and instituted a new set of policies putting some teeth behind the equal treatment of women employees. Shortly after this, negotiations made headway and a new contract was signed. It is most important when you see a minority group standing staunchly on a point, to pursue an understanding of what is driving their stand. You may find an underlying element that has not been accounted for.

"In developing consensus, instead of dismissing the viewpoint of others, seek to find what is behind strongly held viewpoints; there are usually deep beliefs driving motivation. In order to find out what those beliefs might be, ask persons representing the viewpoint to explain the thinking and feelings behind their position. Listen "actively," asking further questions as they clarify, while reflecting back understanding and empathy (don't cross-examine) in the hope that they will trust you enough go deeper and reveal the core of their concerns."

Ken: "One spring, our building-based language arts coordinator suggested that we survey the staff to confirm our belief that the decoding assessment component we had been piloting had sufficient faculty support (i.e., that we truly had reached consensus on this aspect of our goal). We could then chalk up another area as 'done' and move on. We planned to share what we assumed were going to be the positive results of the survey at an upcoming faculty meeting.

"To our surprise, the survey showed we were nowhere near consensus. A substantial number of faculty expressed dissatisfaction with use of the pilot assessment—both on their survey and at the staff meeting when we shared the results. The coordinator was disheartened because it *felt* like 'everyone' was opposed to the assessment, and it appeared as if we were going to have to start all over again.

"The coordinator and I met again, and we decided to talk individually with teachers whose survey responses were negative to dig a little deeper. As a result of these meetings, we found that the dissatisfaction with the new assessment practice was related to a few specific implementation issues that could be fixed.

"*Most surprising was the discovery that the negativity did not extend to the overall worth or usefulness of the assessment itself. They were not rejecting the assessment method. In fact, they liked it! (It is important to dig for all the facts and not make assumptions.)*"

Appendix C

Opening Exercises

1. "Ways Organizations Are Focused"
2. "An Ordinary Paper Cup"
3. "Best Workplace"

The following exercises assist in establishing felt-need while helping participants get in touch with their highest ideals and best aspirations for the school. Read these exercises and utilize those that feel "right" to you and can best fit into your schedule.

EXERCISE #1: "WAYS ORGANIZATIONS ARE FOCUSED"
(APPROXIMATELY 15 MINUTES)

Hand out the list of the "Seven Ways Organizations Can Be Focused," each with an underlined space beside it.

Seven Ways Organizations Can Be Focused

1. Many individual focuses _____
2. Pleasing the boss _____
3. Doing what we have always done _____
4. Getting through the day _____
5. Reacting to events/putting out fires _____
6. Controlled by the bottom line/budget _____

7. Doing what we see as best for students/what we agree to do together

_____

Tell the group that most organizations find themselves in each of these focuses at one time or another. Ask *them to place beside each focus the percentage of time they believe your school spends in each focus.* All you need is a rough estimate or guess. Individual percentages should roughly add up to 100 percent. When they have written their percentages, get a rough idea of an average for each by going through the seven focuses one at a time asking them to raise their hands if their percentage for that approach is in the category you call for—for instance, 0–10 percent, 11–20 percent, 21–30 percent, etc. Assign a rough percentage estimation for each focus, from the midpoint of the percentage range that produces the most hands at any one time. Review the percentages when you have gone through all seven.

Then ask the question, *"Which of these focus areas do you think correlates highest with a sense of accomplishment and job satisfaction?"* The group will select #7. Then the facilitator observes that according to the group's responses, we presently spend ___ percent of our time in this focus (it may be low). Then ask the question, *"Could spending more time in this organizational focus mean increasing job satisfaction and a sense of accomplishment?"* It is then logical to ask, *"If spending time in the areas of what is best for students and on goals that we agree to do together is a key to increased accomplishment and job satisfaction, how can we get more time in those areas?"*

Conclude by noting that the exercise is meant to show why we are opening a dialogue about a new and expanded process for improvement planning (i.e., because *this way of planning will allow us to spend more time and put more emphasis on " what is best for students and what we agree to do together"—and because doing that will increase our job satisfaction and sense of accomplishment*).

EXERCISE #2: "AN ORDINARY PAPER CUP" (ESTIMATED TIME 10–15 MINUTES)

The facilitator shows the group an ordinary paper drinking cup and says, *"I'm going to give you one minute to see how many uses you can write down for a cup like this. The uses can be creative as long as the cup could really be used in that way."* The group is timed for one minute. At the end of the minute, find out who has the most possible uses. Ask that individual to read his or her list and ask everyone else to cross off duplicate items on their lists.

List the uses on a board, flip chart, or projected computer. Take the next person with the most remaining uses, and so on, until all uses created by the group have been listed. *The conclusion made by the facilitator is that the most uses any one person had was ____ uses (let's say twelve), but the group as a whole came up with ____ uses (let's say thirty). Note that three or four to one (group compared to individual) is the typical outcome.* Then the facilitator asks, "What does this exercise tell us about using teamwork to plan school improvement?" We would hope that discussion would focus around the question, *"If we could work together smoothly and efficiently, wouldn ' t it be better for planning improvements to have three times the creativity, three times the input of options for solution, and three times the input as to how to make the best decisions we can for our students?"*

Let them come to the conclusions; don't just state the conclusions and ask them to agree with you. Conclude, if they haven't said it already (if so, repeat it), that this exercise is offered to explain *why we not only want to spend more time improving the school (previous exercise), but why we will accomplish more in that improvement effort working as a team.* It demonstrates why "we" is better than "me."

EXERCISE #3: "BEST WORKPLACE" (ESTIMATED TIME 45 MINUTES)

Move quickly from any of the earlier exercises to talking about the "knowledge base" that exists in this group. It is another reason that teamwork is so powerful. The meeting facilitator says, *"Look to your left and right. What is sitting next to you in the form of your coworkers is every book they have ever read, every course they have ever taken, every experience they have ever had, and every wise person who ever gave them advice. Our collective learning and experiences are a tremendous 'knowledge base.' Let's do an exercise called 'Best Workplace' to demonstrate the power of this knowledge base."* Give the group a few minutes to individually jot down the characteristics of the best place they ever worked. Broaden the exercise to include any team, community, or voluntary organization that they have *personally* experienced. Invite volunteers to share by asking them the following: *"Tell us what type of organization it was and name one or two characteristics that made it a special place."* List the characteristics in some visible format.

When you have a sufficient list and people are done offering examples, review the list and make the following observation: *"This list is an outstanding profile of the characteristics of an exceptional organization."* (You will really be amazed what a complete and excellent list of characteristics of a well-run organization your group will compile.) *"This thorough definition has been here in this group the whole time—along with a great deal of other valuable knowledge and abilities; what we need is a system that allows us to efficiently access this knowledge base and tap into those abilities. That's what a good system of collaborative improvement does."*

Appendix D

The Working Values

A team's working environment is formed by the manner in which each member participates in the process. The goal of these working values is to help members create a working environment which is productive and rewarding as well as enjoyable.

BE ENCOURAGING TO OTHERS:
Receiving and giving encouragement helps us to do our best. If we recognize the efforts of others and encourage each other, we will feel good about working together and are more likely to produce an excellent result.

GIVE OTHERS THE RESPECT WE WANT TO RECEIVE:
When we speak we want others to listen to us, having an open mind to the ideas we are presenting. We should offer others the same openness that we want. In such an atmosphere, ideas flow freely, making the process more productive.

MAINTAIN A POSITIVE ATTITUDE:
Keeping a positive attitude in the face of negativity creates an environment that is positive, productive, and successful. Reacting negatively to a problem or situation only escalates it.

BE HONEST AND OPEN:
Members must be able to take action on the basis of information provided by other team members. Hidden agendas break trust and destroy the team's ability to interact successfully.

NOT MY IDEAS, BUT THE BEST IDEAS:
The team process is a search for improvements that work best. Come to the table in pursuit of the best ideas. If others can improve upon our ideas, we should encourage them to do so.

MAKE THE TEAM'S TASK OUR HIGHEST PRIORITY:
Successful teams are those that truly come together behind a mutually shared vision and goals. For this to occur, the task of the team must be given precedence over the many different personal priorities that also motivate us.

TRUST GOES BEYOND THE MEETING:
Be loyal to those not present at all times. Establish working relationships built on trust and integrity. Respect for others builds a sense of confidence and community.

FOCUS ON LISTENING, NOT JUST HEARING:
To listen actively is to make an effort to understand and respect another person's thoughts and feelings. If we are merely hearing, we may be thinking about our next response and miss an opportunity for understanding.

TRY FIRST TO UNDERSTAND, THEN TO BE UNDERSTOOD:
What we already know may only be part of the information we need to make wise decisions. When we listen to others first, more facts and points of view become available, enabling us to make better choices and develop team consensus.

PRESET SOLUTIONS HINDER PROGRESS:
A key to successful planning is for members to state their interests and concerns while being open and flexible as to how those interests will be achieved - leaving the process open to creative solutions.

BE TOUGH ON THE ISSUES, EASY ON THE PEOPLE:
Say what you mean, but don't say it mean. Standing up for good ideas adds real value to the process. Making our remarks personal sabotages the team's task and pushes the team toward gridlock. Focus on the issue while avoiding the personal.

AVOID INTERPRETING OTHER'S MOTIVATIONS:
People will usually allow us our own thoughts and feelings without becoming defensive. It is effective to talk about what we think and feel and avoid interpreting the actions and motivations of others. People resent it and become defensive when we act as if we understand their thoughts better than they do.

BLAME NO ONE, FIX THE PROBLEM:
Blame adds a second problem to the original problem. Staying respectful and on the side of others, even when they make a mistake, is critically important to good, long-term, working relationships.

RESPECT DIVERSITY:
Diversity contributes to the strength of our collective efforts. We each have a unique contribution to make and everyone's contribution is to be honored. We will respect the diverse paths to excellence.

Figure D.1 Working Values

Appendix E

Examples of the One-Page Improvement Plan

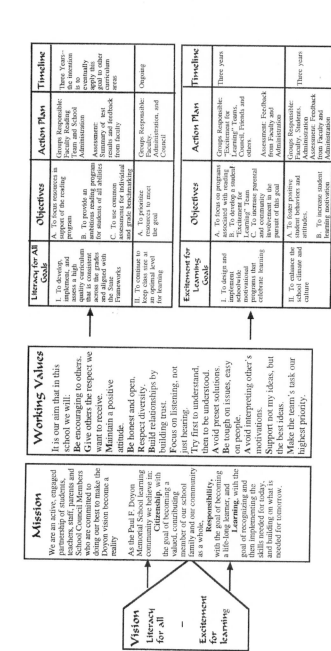

Mission

We are an active, engaged partnership of students, teachers, staff, parents and School Council Members who are committed to doing our best to make the Doyon vision become a reality

As the Paul F. Doyon Memorial School learning community we believe in: **Citizenship**, with the goal of becoming a valued, contributing member of our school family and our community as a whole, **Responsibility**, with the goal of becoming a life-long learner, and **Learning**, with the goal of recognizing and then implementing the skills needed for today, and building on what is needed for tomorrow.

Working Values

It is our aim that in this school we will:
Be encouraging to others.
Give others the respect we want to receive.
Maintain a positive attitude.
Be honest and open.
Respect diversity.
Build relationships by building trust.
Focus on listening, not just hearing.
Try first to understand, then to be understood.
Avoid preset solutions.
Be tough on issues, easy on people.
Avoid interpreting other's motivations.
Support not my ideas, but the best ideas.
Make the team's task our highest priority.

Vision
Literacy for all
–
Excitement for learning

Literacy for All Goals	Objectives	Action Plan	Timeline
I. To develop, implement, and assess a high quality curriculum that is consistent across the grades and aligned with the State Frameworks	A. To focus resources in support of the reading program B. To provide an ambitious reading program for students of all abilities C. To use common assessments for individual and grade benchmarking	Groups Responsible: Faculty Reading Team and School Administration Assessment: Summary of test results and feedback from faculty	Three Years—the intention is to eventually apply this goal to other curriculum areas
II. To continue to keep class size at an optimal level for learning	A. To prioritize resources to meet the goal	Groups Responsible: Faculty, Administration, and Council	Ongoing

Excitement for Learning Goals	Objectives	Action Plan	Timeline
I. To design and implement schoolwide motivational programs that celebrate learning	A. To focus on programs associated with reading B. To develop a student "Excitement for Learning" Team C. To increase parental and community involvement in the pursuit of this goal	Groups Responsible: "Excitement for Learning" Teams, Council, Friends and others. Assessment: Feedback from Faculty and Administration	Three years
II. To enhance the school climate and culture	A. To foster positive student behaviors and attitudes, B. To increase student learning motivation	Groups Responsible: Faculty, Students, Administration Assessment: Feedback from Faculty and Administration	Three years

Figure E.1 Doyon School Improvement Plan, 1997–1998

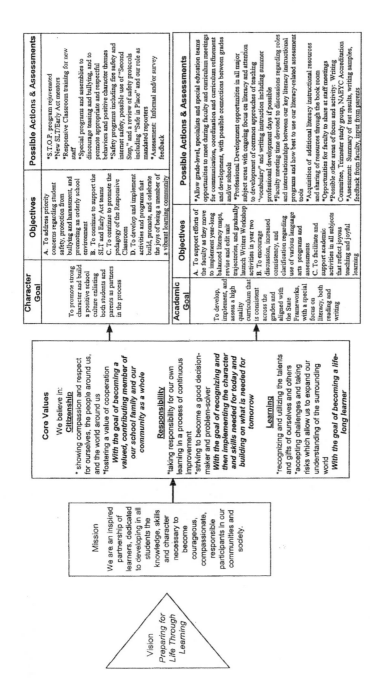

Vision
Preparing for Life Through Learning

Mission
We are an inspired partnership of learners, dedicated to developing in all students the knowledge, skills and character necessary to become courageous, compassionate, responsible participants in our communities and society.

Core Values

We believe in:

Citizenship
* showing compassion and respect for ourselves, the people around us, and the world around us
*fostering a value of cooperation
With the goal of becoming a valued, contributing member of our school family and our community as a whole

Responsibility
*taking responsibility for our own learning in a process of continuous improvement
*striving to become a good decision-maker and problem-solver
With the goal of recognizing and then implementing the character and skills needed for today and building on what is needed for tomorrow

Learning
*recognizing and utilizing the talents and gifts of ourselves and others
*accepting challenges and taking risks which allow us to expand our understanding of the surrounding world
With the goal of becoming a life-long learner

Character Goal	Objectives	Possible Actions & Assessments
To promote strong character and build a positive school culture enlisting both students and parents as partners in the process	A. To address priority concerns regarding student safety, protection from bullying and harassment, and promoting an orderly school environment B. To continue to support the SLT and Early Act teams C. To continue to promote the pedagogy of the Responsive Classroom D. To develop and implement activities and programs that build, promote, and celebrate the joys of being a member of a vibrant learning community	*S.T.O.P. program rejuvenated *New SLT/Early Act mentors *Responsive Classroom training for new staff *Special programs and assemblies to discourage teasing and bullying, and to promote appropriate and respectful behaviors and positive character themes *Safety programs including fire safety and internet safety, possible use of "Second Step," and a review of safety protocols including "Safe in Place" and our role as mandated reporters *Assessment: Informal and/or survey feedback

Academic Goal	Objectives	Possible Actions & Assessments
To develop, implement, and assess a high quality curriculum that is consistent across the grades and aligned with the State Frameworks, with a special focus on literacy, both reading and writing	A. To support efforts of the faculty as they move to implement year-long balanced literacy maps, revise and edit unit trajectories, and gradually launch Writers Workshop activities in year two B. To encourage discussion, increased consistency, and clarification regarding use of various language arts programs and assessments C. To facilitate and support academic activities in all subjects that reflect joyous teaching and joyful learning	*Allow grade-level, specialists and special education teams opportunities to meet during faculty and curriculum meetings for communication, coordination and curriculum refinement and development, with possible connections between grades and/or schools *Professional Development opportunities in all major subject areas with ongoing focus on literacy and attention to development of common approaches of teaching "vocabulary" and writing instruction including summer professional development days if possible *Faculty meeting time devoted to discussions regarding roles and interrelationships between our key literacy instructional programs and how best to use our literacy-related assessment tools *Acquisition of additional literacy instructional resources and sharing of resources through the book room *Opportunities for faculty to share at staff meetings *Possible other areas of focus and activity: Writing Committee, Trimester study group, NAEYC Accreditation *Assessment: Summary of test results, writing samples, feedback from faculty, input from parents

Figure E.2 Doyon School Improvement Plan, 2007–2009

Appendix F

Vision-Setting Exercises

1. "If Things Went Great"
2. "Quick Prioritization"
3. "Causes of Positive Change"

EXERCISE #1: "IF THINGS WENT GREAT"
(ESTIMATED TIME 1 HOUR)

The "Best Workplace" exercise provides us with an excellent list of characteristics of an outstanding organization. It also starts providing us with a description of what you and your staff will have to do to make yours a great school. The next step is to pose this question: *"Presume that things go great for this school in the next three to five years. At the end of that time the school is doing a truly outstanding job for our students. Close your eyes and visualize that school. Significant improvements have been made.* (Give them a minute.) *What one or two things happened that were most significant to you to make ours a better school for our students?"*

Go around the group asking for answers in short phrases. Record the responses. We are not seeking a long list from any individual, but only the one or two things (at the most) that would have the highest priority (hold the greatest meaning) for each of them. If needed, remind the group that the criterion is "a better school for our students." Do not combine answers unless they are exactly or nearly the same. Be wary of grouping specific comments into general categories lest their meaning become lost. Ask participants what they mean, when meaning is not clear.

What we want is a list of specific and clear actions or areas for improvement that would make this school a better school over the next three to five years. The group will again provide an excellent list of possible actions to improve the school; they know what needs to be done, though they might have to research the best way to do it.

For this exercise, you should end by prioritizing the suggestions. Up to this point, we are only aware that each item on the list is supported by the person who offered the idea. We need to know which of the items are of highest priority to the group. People need the feedback to know if their ideas have wide support, moderate support, or little support. We often use a method of "quick prioritizing" as described below.

After the prioritization exercise, it is a good idea to distribute the results to all participants in a timely manner. Also mention to the group that they will be revisiting these lists when it comes time to set vision, goals, and objectives.

EXERCISE #2: "QUICK PRIORITIZATION"
(ESTIMATED TIME 10 MINUTES)

This prioritization approach works by allowing participants to allot points for about 25 percent of the suggestions. If, for example, the group has generated sixteen suggestions for school improvement, we will allow each individual to assign points to four of the options. Points will be given *inversely* by each person as follows: 4 points for their top choice, 3 for a second choice, 2 for a third choice, and 1 for a fourth choice. Review the list one at a time asking staff to note their top four on a scratch pad.

Remind them before the count begins that their top choice is given four points and their fourth choice one point. Remind them that they can give points to only four items. Go through the list one at a time, tallying points by having them hold up the number of fingers representing the points they are giving that item (i.e., holding up one, two, three, or four fingers, or no fingers if the item is not one of their top four). Count fingers and circle the total for each item one at a time.

At the end, note which three or four items received the most points. There is usually a natural break where one or two stand out or three or four are close and the rest only marginally supported. Conclude by saying, "again we see the knowledge base of this group demonstrated by the group's ability to select focused areas that give direction to our school's future improvement efforts."

EXERCISE #3: "CAUSES OF POSITIVE CHANGE" (ESTIMATED TIME 30 MINUTES)

In this follow-up exercise, we look at the top rated outcomes from the "If Things Went Great" and "Quick Prioritization" exercises and ask what needs to happen for these outcomes to actually occur. Here we are asking participants to go deeper in their thinking from outcomes to causes. For instance, a top outcome of the "If Things Went Great" exercise might be an improvement in standardized test reading scores. Next, we want to understand what actions might lead to such a rise in reading scores (e.g., receiving additional training in some aspect of teaching reading).

The purpose of this exercise is to help us prepare for drafting vision, mission, goals, and objectives. (An alternative would be to hold off on doing this exercise until you began the Phase III goal-setting process, but we present it here as an option. You can revisit these results—or re-do the exercise—as a component of your goal-setting sessions.)

Finding the root causes of positive change is a key to making it happen.

Before beginning this exercise, provide a few minutes of "thinking" time to allow participants to note ideas individually. This encourages people to get to deeper levels of causality. The format "think-write-discuss" can be used with any of the exercises to encourage more analytic thinking—thus allowing quality ideas to have time to surface.

Appendix G

Goal-Setting Exercises

1. "Roundtable Format"
2. "TEAM" Exercise

EXERCISE #1: "ROUNDTABLE FORMAT" (TIME DEPENDS ON TOPIC/NUMBER OF PEOPLE)

This discussion format is especially helpful in encouraging substantive input from as many individuals as possible. It is a way to allow each person even in a fairly large group an opportunity to address the topic at hand. Chairs are arranged in a circle. The facilitator brings the group's attention to the focus topic for the session. An example as related to goal accomplishment might be, "*If things went great in our school over the next five years, what positive changes would have benefited students most?*" Frame the topic in a manner that clearly indicates the focus for the session.

Share the ground rules:

- Each person will have "X" amount of time to talk.
- We will go around the circle in order.
- You may "pass"; we will come back to you if you wish.
- Keep the working values in mind.
- No out-of-turn interruptions or comments permitted.
- If we have time, we will go around again, allowing cross-talk and providing additional opportunity for "piggybacking" of ideas.

Give the group a minute or two to reflect, and then ask for a volunteer to begin addressing the topic or just assign someone to start. It is helpful to have a "timekeeper" with a second hand or a stopwatch who can provide a *gentle* sound of some kind to chime when a person's time expires. The amount of time you provide each person depends on the length of the meeting and the number of participants. We usually settled on 1–2 minutes. While cross-circle comments are not allowed in the first go-round while another is speaking, the current speaker can reference prior comments either to piggyback ideas or to endorse or offer different views.

A type of "circle dialogue" will emerge the second time around, so it's important to try to plan your time to allow for that. This format encourages people to participate who have good things to add to the discussion but who might otherwise just listen and let others carry the discussion. While you as principal should definitely take a turn as a participant, you should also be looking for emerging areas of agreement. Someone can be recording comments in brief in some sort of display format. It may also be helpful to have a notetaker in the circle briefly record the essence of each comment in written form for analysis afterward.

EXERCISE #2: "TEAM EXERCISE" (ESTIMATED TIME 45 MINUTES)

This exercise is a variation on brainstorming and quick prioritizing exercises. It is worth considering because (a) it is fun, (b) each step is time delimited (minutes allotted are in parentheses following each step) with the objective of completing the entire exercise in one hour, and (c) it's perfect for a first quick sense of a group's *priority areas for improvement*.

Preparation: Prepare sets of index cards, four cards to a set. To determine how many sets simply divide the size of the group by four. So if there are 24 people in the group, you will ready six sets of four cards each. Write the same number on each of the four cards in a single set. You should now have four cards with the number 1, four cards with the number 2, etc. Now go back to the #1's and write a "T" on one card, an "E" on another, an "A" on the next and an "M" on the last. Do the same for the set of #2 cards and for the remaining sets 3–6. The four number ones will now be labeled 1-T, 1-E, 1-A, 1-M, and so forth for the other numbers.

Shuffle the entire stack and hand one card to each person as they enter the meeting.

1. Introduction of the activity and the process (8 minutes).

2. Introduce a question as the main item for the agenda, such as "*If things went great in our school over the next five years, what positive changes would have benefited students the most?*" (2 minutes).

3. Form groups of four by the given card numbers—this will cause a few minutes of movement as all "ones" find each other and sit together, all the "twos," etc., according to the cards distributed. Each group receives a pad of stickies (3 minutes).

4. A flip chart page or screen (which up to this point hasn't been visible) is unveiled and the following jobs/roles are assigned according to the letters (1 minute).

   - T: Timekeeper—tries to keep the group to the time allowed.
   - E: Recorder—posts stickies on the master chart as per #11 below.
   - A: Gatekeeper—encourages the group to stay focused on the tasks.
   - M: Facilitator—starts the process, keeps it going, and counts the tallies as per #10 below.

5. Each participant individually jots down several personal answers to the "if things went great" question on *separate* stickies (4 minutes).

6. Each group goes around and each of the four persons in the group places what they think is their single-most important response in the center of the group's table (2 minutes).

7. Each group goes around again and each person contributes their second-best idea to the middle (2 minutes).

8. Each group looks over the eight stickies in the center of their respective tables and combines identical or overlapping topics if both contributors agree that they are the same (3 minutes).

9. Each individual next privately prioritizes the three stickies from the eight in the center of their table that are most important to them and, again privately, assigns three points to the *most* important, two points to the next most important, and one point to their third choice (3 minutes).

10. Quick Prioritization: The facilitator points to each sticky and members hold up fingers to show if they gave it points (4 minutes).

11. The Recorder (the "E" person from each group) moves to post the group's two top-weighted stickies onto the whole group's master flip chart, noting on the sticky how many points each received (3 minutes).

12. The *whole* group (i.e., everyone in the room) looks over the stickies on the master chart, combining them with permission of the groups who posted them (4 minutes).

13. The *whole* group then does a collective 3-2-1 weighted quick prioritization of all the stickies posted on the combined master chart (4 minutes).

Appendix H

Planning and Problem-Solving Tools

1. "The Planning Process Steps Chart"
2. "The Problem-Solving Steps Chart"

Appendix H

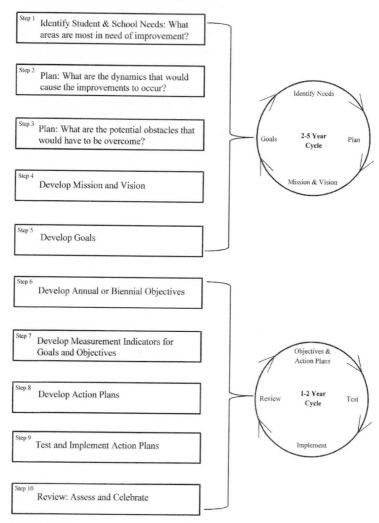

Figure H.1 Planning Process Steps

Step 1	Step 2	Step 3	Step 4	Step5
Understand the Problem	Identify Causes	Determine the Best Solution	Implement and Measure	Evaluate
1. Define the problem. 2. Ask "Is this a problem worth pursuing?" 3. Consider how progress can be measured.	4. Identify the suspected causes of the problem. 5. Prioritize the causes. 6. Identify a cause to address that promises the best results.	7. Reference others who have had success addressing this problem. 8. Develop solution options. 9. Discuss the pros and cons of options. 10. Select the best solution. 11. Test the solution. 12. If positive, proceed. If negative, target a different cause.	13. Agree on a measurement tool and take a baseline reading. 14. Implement the chosen solution throughout the organization.	15. Follow up, track and assess. 16. Periodically report progress. 17. Celebrate the achievement of milestones. 18 Go back and look at other causes of the problem to see if they offer value for time. Otherwise go on to the next problem.

Figure H.2 Problem-Solving Process Steps

Appendix I

Sample Survey Questions

For many of the survey questions we used a ratings scale similar to the one below:
(Circle the number closest to your viewpoint.)
1. (A Great Deal)   2. (Usually)   3. (Somewhat)   4. (Not At All)

STUDENT SURVEY QUESTIONS

All Grade Levels

1. I pause and think about consequences before making decisions.
2. Most students will treat you well if you treat them well.
3. I prefer to say positive things about other people.
4. I work well with others.
5. I can talk to others about how I feel.
6. I can tell how others are feeling by observing them.
7. I organize time in my day to do my homework.
8. I set high standards for myself.
9. I keep trying to succeed even if I fail at times.
10. There are some things that I am really good at.
11. I am hopeful about my future.
12. I do my best at my schoolwork.
13. This school is a good place for me to come each school day.
14. Students like this school.
15. I feel safe here at school.
16. I feel respected by the other students.

151

17. Adults in our school are supportive and helpful.

18. Teachers here help students who need extra help.

19. In this school there are places to go for help and advice.

20. Classroom lessons here are well organized and generally interesting.

21. Classroom lessons here are often connected to real-life examples.

22. I am comfortable using computers and other technology .

23. This school gives me opportunities to participate in activities.

24. The Ipswich schools are providing me with a good education.

25. I am confident about going on to the next level of my education.

26. At our school there are clear disciplinary rules and consequences.

27. When problems arise at our school, they are dealt with fairly.

28. I think it is important to stop bullying and put-downs.

29. Most students will speak up and try to stop bullying.

30. I often feel sad or depressed.

31. I have been excluded from groups.

32. Bullying has happened to me this year.

33. Because I was afraid of being picked on, some days I did not want to come to school.

34. Violence and bullying are problems in our school.

35. Where does bullying happen? Circle all that apply: Nowhere; Classroom; Recess; Lunch; Bus; Hallways; Bathrooms; Online.

36. I find my school work this year to be: (Circle One) Very easy; Somewhat easy; Just right; Somewhat hard; Very hard.

Written Questions for All Student Surveys

37. The things I like most about our school are:

    38. The things I would improve about our school are:

Additional Middle and High School Questions

39. Our school strictly enforces drug and alcohol prohibitions.

40. There is peer pressure to take drugs or alcohol.

41. Drug, alcohol, and tobacco use is a significant problem among students.

42. I have been offered illegal drugs or alcohol on school property.

43. Pressure to engage in sexual activity is a significant problem in our school.

Additional Bullying Questions

1. Bullying in the form of *hitting or physical hurting* has happened to me in this year.

2. Bullying in the form of *repeated mean teasing (name calling, making fun of, belittling)* has happened to me this year.

3. Bullying in the form of *repeated threats to hurt me* has happened this school year.

4. Bullying in the form of *taking away my property by force* has happened to me this school year.

5. Bullying in the form of *saying untrue things behind my back, gossiping, hurting my reputation* has happened to me this school year.

6. Bullying in the form of *purposely excluding me from groups* has happened this year.

TEACHER SURVEY QUESTIONS

At our school, teaching positions are structured to allow teachers

1. to discover and try new ideas;
2. to experience job satisfaction;
3. to experience opportunities for professional growth;
4. to participate actively in decisions about teaching and learning;
5. time for classroom preparation;
6. time for grade/department planning; and
7. time for cross grade/department planning.

In our school, we:

8. have a clear sense of what we want to accomplish;
9. work together well, have good teamwork;
10. provide opportunities for teachers to get feedback about how well we are doing;
11. show appreciation for the efforts of faculty;
12. work with discipline and disruption issues as to reduce their frequency in the future;
13. have clear expectations for student accountability and responsibility;
14. have administrative support in dealing with discipline issues;
15. feel supported by building administration;
16. are flexible and creative in meeting student needs;
17. have clear learning expectations for each grade/subject;
18. have an academic plan from grade to grade;
19. have accurate measurement of literacy skills from grade to grade;
20. have sufficient intervention strategies for students who are behind;
21. have mutual respect among staff and faculty;
22. have mutual respect among students;
23. have an attitude of interest and effort among students.

Teacher Survey Written Questions

1. What one area of potential improvement do you think would produce the most beneficial results for students in this school?

2. What steps or keys do you see as important for accomplishing the above area of improvement? How would you see it being done?

FAMILY SURVEY

My child is in grade _____.

1. Does your student enjoy coming to school? ___ Yes ___ No
If the answer is "No," what are the reasons?

2. Does your student feel safe at school? ___Very Safe, ___Safe,
___Somewhat Unsafe, ___Unsafe
If your answer is "Somewhat Unsafe" or "Unsafe," what are the reasons?

3. What is your priority for your child's years at our school?

4. What do you like most about the school?

5. What can be improved?

6. Would you like to make specific comments about

- school culture and climate?
- support and cooperation of administrators, teachers, and staff?
- educational programs?

7. Have you been involved in volunteering or helping at the school?
___Yes ___ No ___ No, but I will in the future

8. I have volunteered or helped by
_____

Acknowledgments

Ken: I would like to thank my parents for their love, and for forgiving me for quitting law school. They both passed away in 2010 and I miss them. I would be remiss if I failed to recognize the contribution of the educators who over the years helped me grow both as a person and as a professional: To my mentors at the University of Colorado Graduate School of Education, Haz Wuben, Myrle Hemenway, and Russ Meyers; to my fieldwork supervisor, Claudine Garby; and to superintendents Dan Cabral, Gerry Bourgeois, Rick Korb, and especially Dick Thompson—your tutelage, your encouragement, and your confidence in me has meant everything. I extend my thanks and admiration both to my administrative colleagues, Carolyn Davis, Barry Cahill, Cheryl Forester-Cahill, Steven Fortado, and Diana Minton—affectionately referred to as the "Camelot Team"—with whom I had the pleasure of working for more than a decade, and to the faculty and staff of the Paul F. Doyon Memorial School in Ipswich, Massachusetts, whose dedicated work on behalf of students went beyond anything any administrator could have required of them. My gratitude goes as well to my coauthors Joe Salah and Nels Gustafson, who helped me find "the path forward" whenever I stalled, and to the fine folks at Rowman & Littlefield, who have given us an opportunity to share what we have learned. Finally, an ocean of love to my wife, Ruth, for her patience and support during the work on this book—you are my partner, my inspiration, and my *ikigai*.

Nels: My gratitude goes to my coauthors Joe Salah and Ken Cooper, who did the majority of the work that made this book possible. I would be remiss if I failed to take this opportunity to recognize the contribution of the many people at Sylvania who provided expertise and shared knowledge with me during my years working there. That knowledge allowed me to contribute to this effort to help schools. To the people we worked with in the Ipswich schools, I wish to say thanks. Most importantly, I wish to thank my wife, Suzanne, and my sons Marc and Derek for their love and support over the years.

Joe: To the God of my belief for planting in my heart the lifelong question I've pursued: "Who are we and why do we do what we do?" To my grandparents and parents for teaching me what family means and how to be an honorable person. To Ken Cooper for never losing his fervor or ideals, and for applying the concepts of quality management and collaborative leadership so sincerely and intelligently that he proved they work. To Nels Gustafson for copiously sharing ideas and advice, and being such a great example of living with generosity and wisdom. To Sandy Campbell, our friend and former partner. To Dick Thompson, Rick Korb, Diana Minton, Caroline Davis, Cheryl Forster-Cahill, Barry Cahill, Sheila McAdams, Dave Archambault, Sheila Conley, Dave Dalton, Meredith Joss, and Kathy McMahon, the administrators of the Ipswich schools who worked with us, for always seeking what is best for kids, and doing it with a willing spirit and a great attitude. To the group of teacher leaders in the Ipswich schools, too numerous to mention individually, whose leadership was indispensable, and who made the administrators truly leaders of leaders. To my wife, Nancy, who has walked lovingly with me, and often times ahead of me, for over forty years on a path seeking to know the truth and to understand how to live a life of love.

Bibliography

Begley, Sharon. *Train Your Mind, Change Your Brain: How a New Science Reveals Our Extraordinary Potential to Transform Ourselves*. New York: Random House/Ballantine, 2008.

Cruikshank, Jeffrey, and Lawrence Susskind. *Breaking the Impasse: Consensual Approaches to Resolving Public Disputes*. New York: Perseus/Basic Books, 1987.

Csikszentmihalyi, Mihaly. *Flow: The Psychology of Optimal Experience*. New York: Harper-Collins, 1990.

Daniels, Aubrey C. *Bringing Out the Best in People: How to Apply the Astonishing Power of Positive Reinforcement*. New York: McGraw-Hill, 1999.

Deming, W. Edwards. *The New Economics for Industry, Government, Education*. 2nd ed. Cambridge, MA: MIT Press, 2000.

———. *Out of the Crisis*. Boston: MIT Press, 2000.

Deutschman, Alan. *Change or Die: The Three Keys to Change at Work and in Life*. New York: HarperCollins, 2007.

Dispenza, Joe. *Evolve Your Brain: The Science of Changing Your Mind*. Deerfield Beach, FL: Health Communications, 2007.

Drucker, Peter F. "The New Society of Organizations." In *Quality Goes to School*, edited by Lewis A. Rhodes, 9–18. Arlington, VA: American Association of School Administrators, 1994.

Fischer, Louis. *Gandhi: His Life and Message for the World*. New York: Penguin, 1982.

Fisher, Roger, William L. Ury, and Bruce Patton. *Getting to Yes: Negotiating Agreement Without Giving In*. New York: Penguin, 1991.

Gallwey, W. Timothy, Zach Kleiman, and Pete Carroll. *The Inner Game of Tennis: The Classic Guide to the Mental Side of Peak Performance*. New York: Random House, 2008.

Glasser, William. *Control Theory: A New Explanation of How We Control Our Lives*. New York: Harper & Row, 1985.

———. *Control Theory Manager*. New York: HarperCollins, 1994.

———. *The Quality School: Managing Students without Coercion*. New York: HarperCollins, 1998.

Goleman, Daniel. *Emotional Intelligence*. New York: Bantam, 1995.

Losada, Marcial, and Emily Heaphy. "The Role of Positivity and Connectivity in the Performance of Business Teams: A Nonlinear Dynamics Model." *American Behavioral Scientist* 47, no.6 (2004): 740–65.

Massachusetts Educational Reform Act of 1993. Massachusetts General Law, chapter 71.

Montgomery, William L. *Power-Up Teams and Tools for Process Improvement and Problem Solving*. 2nd ed. Pittstown, NJ: Montgomery Group, 1999.

Ndoye, Abdou, Scott R. Imig, and Michele A. Parker. "Empowerment, Leadership, and Teachers' Intentions to Stay or Leave the Profession or Their Schools." *Journal of School Choice* 4, no. 2 (2010): 174–90.

Pink, Daniel H. *Drive: The Surprising Truth about What Motivates Us.* New York: Penguin, 2009.

Ravitch, Diane. *The Death and Life of the Great American School System: How Testing and Choice Are Undermining Education.* New York: Perseus/Basic Books, 2010.

Ryan, Kathleen D., and Daniel K. Oestreich. *Driving Fear Out of the Workplace: Creating the High-Trust, High Performance Organization.* San Francisco: Jossey-Bass, 1998.

Schmoker, Mike, and Richard Wilson. "Transforming Schools through Total Quality Education." In *Quality Goes to School,* edited by Lewis A. Rhodes, 9–18. Arlington, VA: American Association of School Administrators, 1994.

Senge, Peter M. *The Fifth Discipline: The Art and Practice of the Learning Organization.* New York: Random House/Doubleday, 2006.

Senge, Peter, and Colleen Lannon-Kim. "Recapturing the Spirit of Learning through a Systems Approach." In *Quality Goes to School,* edited by Lewis A. Rhodes, 60–65. Arlington, VA: American Association of School Administrators, 1994.

Tribus, Myron. "TQM in Education." In *Quality Goes to School,* edited by Lewis A. Rhodes, 37–40. Arlington VA: American Association of School Administrators, 1994.

Tzu, Lao. *The Complete Works of Lao Tzu.* Translated by Hua-Ching Ni. Los Angeles: Seven-Star Communications, 1995.

Ury, William. *Getting Past No: Negotiating in Difficult Situations.* New York: Bantam, 1993.

Weber, Karl. *Waiting for Superman: How We Can Save America's Failing Public Schools.* New York: Public Affairs, 2010.

Index

About the Authors

Dr. Kenneth B. Cooper is a retired educator with thirty-nine years of professional experience. For twenty-two of those years he served as principal of the Paul F. Doyon Memorial School in Ipswich, Massachusetts.

He has addressed groups including the National Association of Elementary School Principals (NAESP), the American Association of School Administrators (AASA), and Dr. Willard Daggett's Model Schools Conferences on topics including instructional innovation, integration of technology, and creating organizational cultures that support organizational change.

Ken earned a BA in sociology from Dartmouth College, an MA in elementary education from Lesley University, and a doctorate in school administration from the University of Colorado. His doctoral thesis was a statistical analysis of the interpersonal relationships of teachers, parents, and students. He lives in Ipswich, Massachusetts, with his wife, Ruth, and their two cats.

Mr. Nels S. Gustafson is retired after close to thirty years with GTE/Sylvania Corporation in the field of human resources. Nels served as director of human resources and chief labor negotiator for Sylvania.

In addition to holding various positions of increasing responsibility, he was instrumental in the implementation of the Total Quality initiatives that included employee and management training and related organizational changes. This experience contributed greatly to many of the concepts presented in this book.

Nels earned his BA degree from Otterbein College in psychology. He also is a graduate of the Sylvania Human Resources Program. He lives in Conway, New Hampshire, with his wife, Suzanne.

Joseph G. Salah has been an educational consultant specializing in school improvement for the past nineteen years. Over his prior working life he has served as an officer in the U.S. Marines; a city councilor, assistant city manager, and charter commission chair in Gloucester, Massachusetts; president and executive director of the Massachusetts–New Hampshire Thoroughbred Horsemen's Association; and as a co-owner of several businesses.

He has a deep interest in leadership, working relationships, and the process of behavioral change. An active and respected member of his community and church, he has been involved for more than thirty years in various charitable and nonprofit efforts.

Joe is a graduate of Boston University with a degree in business administration. He earned two master's degrees from Salem State University—one in Education, and one in History/American Studies. He lives in Ipswich, Massachusetts, with his wife, Nancy.